Juvenal *Satires*

The following titles are available from Bloomsbury for the OCR specifications in Latin and Greek for examinations from June 2024 to June 2026

Cicero *Pro Caelio*: A Selection, with introduction, commentary notes and vocabulary by Georgina Longley

Juvenal *Satires*: A Selection, with introduction, commentary notes and vocabulary by John Godwin

Ovid *Fasti*: A Selection, with introduction, commentary notes and vocabulary by Robert Cromarty

Letters of Pliny: A Selection, with introduction, commentary notes and vocabulary by Carl Hope

Tacitus *Annals* XII: A Selection, with introduction, commentary notes and vocabulary by Simon Allcock

Tacitus *Annals* XIV: A Selection, with introduction, commentary notes and vocabulary by John Storey

Virgil *Aeneid* II: A Selection, with introduction, commentary notes and vocabulary by Dominic Jones

OCR Anthology for Classical Greek GCSE, covering the prescribed texts by Euripides, Herodotus, Homer and Xenophon, with introduction, commentary notes and vocabulary by Judith Affleck and Clive Letchford

OCR Anthology for Classical Greek AS and A Level, covering the prescribed texts by Aristophanes, Euripides, Herodotus, Homer, Plato and Plutarch, with introduction, commentary notes and vocabulary by Sam Baddeley, Benedict Gravell, Charlie Paterson, Stuart R. Thomson, Neil Treble and Chris Tudor

Online resources to accompany this book are available at bloomsbury.pub/OCR-editions-2024-2026. If you experience any problems, please contact Bloomsbury at: onlineresources@bloomsbury.com

Juvenal *Satires*:
A Selection

6: 1–113, 242–305, 352–65, 398–412
14: 1–33 (*animos auctoribus*),
74 (*serpente ciconia*)–232
15: 27–92

With introduction, commentary notes and
vocabulary by John Godwin

BLOOMSBURY ACADEMIC
LONDON · NEW YORK · OXFORD · NEW DELHI · SYDNEY

BLOOMSBURY ACADEMIC
Bloomsbury Publishing Plc
50 Bedford Square, London, WC1B 3DP, UK
1385 Broadway, New York, NY 10018, USA
29 Earlsfort Terrace, Dublin 2, Ireland

BLOOMSBURY, BLOOMSBURY ACADEMIC and the Diana logo are
trademarks of Bloomsbury Publishing Plc

First published in Great Britain 2023

Cover design: Terry Woodley
Cover image: Ranko Maras / Alamy Stock Photo

A catalogue record for this book is available from the British Library.

A catalog record for this book is available from the Library of Congress.

ISBN: PB: 978-1-3501-5652-4
       ePDF: 978-1-3501-5654-8
       eBook: 978-1-3501-5653-1

Typeset by RefineCatch Limited, Bungay, Suffolk
Printed and bound in India

To find out more about our authors and books visit www.bloomsbury.com
and sign up for our newsletters.

Contents

Endorsement statement

The teaching content of this resource is endorsed by OCR for use with specification AS Level Latin (H043) and specification A Level Latin (H443).

All references to assessment, including assessment preparation and practice questions of any format/style are the publisher's interpretation of the specification and are not endorsed by OCR.

This resource was designed for use with the version of the specification available at the time of publication. However, as specifications are updated over time, there may be contradictions between the resource and the specification, therefore please use the information on the latest specification and Sample Assessment Materials at all times when ensuring students are fully prepared for their assessments.

Endorsement indicates that a resource is suitable to support delivery of an OCR specification, but it does not mean that the endorsed resource is the only suitable resource to support delivery, or that it is required or necessary to achieve the qualification.

OCR recommends that teachers consider using a range of teaching and learning resources based on their own professional judgement for their students' needs. OCR has not paid for the production of this resource, nor does OCR receive any royalties from its sale. For more information about the endorsement process, please visit the OCR website.

Preface

This book is intended to assist students preparing for public examinations in Latin who are required to study this text, but it can of course be used by any students of Latin who have mastered the basics and who are now ready to start reading some Latin verse and developing their skills and their understanding. The notes assume that the reader has studied the Latin language roughly as far as GCSE, but the vocabulary list glosses every word in the text and the Introduction assumes that the reader is coming to Juvenal for the very first time. I have printed third declension accusative plurals as *-es* rather than *-is* for clarity. The commentary seeks to elucidate the background and the literary features of this highly artistic text, while also helping the reader to understand how the Latin words fit together into their sentences. Further commentary notes and more information on related topics may be found on the webpages which accompany this volume.

My thanks are due above all to Alice Wright, Georgina Leighton and their team at Bloomsbury who have been a model of efficiency and enthusiasm and a delight to write for. My thanks also go to Lindsay and Patricia Watson in Sydney and Christine Schmitz in Münster who read the commentary in draft form and made many acute suggestions for improving it. I am also grateful to the anonymous OCR reviewers who read the whole of this book and made many highly useful comments which saved me from error as well as pointing me towards a better reading of the text.

John Godwin
Shrewsbury 2023

Introduction

Juvenal and his times

Almost nothing is known about the life of Decimus Iunius Iuvenalis, the man who wrote some of the most memorable phrases in Latin. Three poems by his contemporary Martial describe him as a 'friend' (VII.24.1), as 'eloquent' (*facundus* VII.91.1) and living the life of a city *cliens* (XII.18) so we know that he was known to (at least one) fellow-poet – but witty ironic epigram is not the most reliable of historical sources on a person's life and circumstances. He does not dedicate his work to a patron (unlike Virgil and Horace), so we can surmise that he was rich enough not to need financial support. He was born somewhere between CE 55 and 68: he refers (4.153) to the murder of the emperor Domitian which took place in CE 96 and also alludes (1.49–50) to events in CE 100, which together securely date his first book of Satires to the early second century CE: there are also chronological markers in *Satire* 15 to the year CE 127.

Beyond that we know almost nothing. The poet refers in his work to a house in Rome (11.171, 190) which was an inheritance (12.87–9) and also to a small farm in Tibur (11.65). There are links between Juvenal's poems and the *Annals* of the historian Tacitus (which suggest that Juvenal knew the historian's work) and he alludes to key individuals in it. There is a temptation to reconstruct the 'life' from the 'art', and plenty of scholars have regarded the *Saturae* as in some ways autobiographical, but modern taste tends to focus on the poetry rather than on the poet; and modern methods of literary analysis of satire draw more attention to the use of role-play, of irony, and of creative imagination in the forming of literary artefacts from the raw material of life. Recent scholarship has placed great emphasis on the poet's anonymity as shown through his manipulation of style and language even when — especially when — he seems to be most open about his feelings.

There is also a need to exercise caution when using the text of a poet such as Juvenal in reconstructing details of the times in which he lived. This author is not composing for an audience such as ourselves, but for his contemporaries, who would not need to be informed of aspects of Roman life with which they were already familiar. Nonetheless, this text has been found useful by historians for the historical events such as comets (6.407) and cannibal feasts in a datable year (15.27) as well as religious practice (6.47–50, 249–50) and social life (e.g. 6.60–70). When it comes to naming individuals, Juvenal has a policy (1.170–1) of only attacking the dead as it is dangerous to attack the living (1.160–70), but he does name a large number of people in these poems and in many cases his audience simply has to know (or guess) who they were. There are names here from history such as Hannibal (6.291), Pyrrhus (14.162), Quintilian (6.75, 6.280), the scholar Celsus (6.245), the eunuch Posides (14.91), Titus Tatius (14.160): and then there are the more obscure targets such as the compulsive builder Caetronius (14.86–95) or the Senator's wife Eppia who ran off with a gladiator (6.82–94). There are some vivid vignettes of crime such as the agricultural imperialism at 14.145–9, and the range of literary and mythological reference makes it obvious that his intended readership (like the poet) had a good education.

Juvenal the poet

It is not, then, as a historical document that Juvenal is read, but rather as a gloriously inventive and interesting text in the tradition of Roman verse satires which dated back several centuries. He gives us vivid images of some extreme human behaviour: look for instance at the rookie soldier losing control of his bowels (14.199–200), the woman bestriding a ship at sea, all nausea forgotten as she follows her lover (6.97–102), the mob violence getting out of hand and turning from fighting to feasting on human flesh (15.27–92). Human emotions are shown in action, and direct speech is often used to voice the (sometimes crazy) attitudes which inspire their actions (see e.g. 6.281–4, 14.191–207). The Eppia passage (6.82–113) is a masterly study of folly and vice, as the narrator both focalizes and satirizes the woman's affection for her gladiator hunk Sergius with the amusing diminutive *Sergiolus* – a diminutive which is all the more amusing as this muscle-bound man is in fact getting on in years (6.105–6). The poet shows us the fighter's face – rubbed raw with his helmet and with a huge lump on his nose – ironically contrasted with Eppia's idealizing view of her man and his 'darling little eye', conveyed in the language of love-elegy and thus adding a further parodic twist to the satire.

Juvenal tells us (1.15–17) that he received a rhetorical education, but his verse is more than versified oratory and his technical skill as a poet is as developed as his mastery of his material. Look for instance at the bathetic use of the 'golden line' (a line with a central verb framed by two nouns and two adjectives) to describe what is anything but golden as at 6.78 and 15.46; or his wonderful use of metrical hiatus at 6.274 where the cheating wife is using her crocodile tears to express anger at her husband's alleged misbehaviour – the lack of elision at the caesura catches her sobbing breaths:

in stati/one su/*a*// *at*/qu' expec/tantibus/ illam.

In the battle scene in *Satire* 15 the poet ironically alludes to epic battle-scenes from Homer and Virgil (15.62–6), with the parody supported by devices such as the bathetic term *coxam* for Aeneas' 'hip' (15.66) to lower the tone. Rhetorical questions are used to express moral outrage: see for instance 14.177–8 ('But what respect for the laws, what apprehension or decency do you ever find in an impatient miser?'), or the mockery of 14.25 ('Do you expect – you moron – that Larga's daughter is not going to commit adultery?'). Enjambement, where a word is held over from the end of one line to the start of the next, is shown to be a powerful satirical tool such as at 6.22; 'it is ancient and long-standing practice, Postumus to … another man's bed' expects a verb like 'respect' but receives instead the euphemistic innuendo *concutere* (to 'rattle'). Juvenal makes good use of diminutive forms to enhance contrast such as at 14.169 where the *vernula* ('little slave') is followed by the *magnis fratribus* ('big brothers') and of course the diminutive is much used in passages advocating the simple life (14.166 *glebula* ('a little clod of earth') and 14.179 ('little cottages' (*casulis*)). The diminutive adds to the theme of degeneration in 15.70, where it is stated that the earth now brings forth men who are 'wicked and weedy' – with the diminutive form *pusillos* an effectively strong word to end the line.

Satire thrives above all on caricature and exaggeration. Look at 14.12 (no child could need 'one thousand tutors'), 14.28 (on the length of the list of a mother's lovers): sometimes (as at 14.114) the poet ironically contrasts the low-level reality with heroic and mythical material. The only way to appreciate the poetry of Juvenal is to read him in Latin and the commentary notes in this book are designed to assist the reader in appreciating all these and many more aspects of this most inventive of poets.

Do the poems have a purpose?

One of the things Roman verse satires claim to do is to criticize, as though it is pleading for a change in human behaviour, because people are being either foolish or positively wicked. On first reading, Juvenal seems to have his own personal axes to grind and is using his poetry to express opinions which he himself held – opinions about women, slaves, rich people, patrons, Greeks, cannibals, modern morals and so on. But are things so simple? Is he actively seeking our agreement with an ethical proposition or is he just using an ethical scenario to show his poetic and rhetorical powers as a writer? Is he 'really' angry or is he just feigning indignation? In the last century, the scholar W.S. Anderson urged that the poet is a performer and that he is creating a character who is the scriptwriter and performer of the words being uttered. This 'character' is referred to by Anderson as a *persona* (which literally means 'mask' and alludes to the theatrical nature of the text) and is the creation of the poet — it is not, therefore, to be taken as identical with the man writing the words on the page. Just as we do not demand total sincerity on the part of a songwriter (who may express feelings in a song which he does not personally share), so also this poet may be conjuring up what are more or less set-piece declamations which are delivered 'in character' behind the mask of savage indignation or shocked outrage which is the satirist's stock in trade.

Clearly, this sort of judgement has to be made in reading many works of literature. When Horace or Catullus express love, we can choose to read the poem as an expression of the poet's 'real' feeling for real people, or else we can read it as a love-poem in the tradition of love poetry and with no need for a real-life situation in the 'real' world behind it. If the writer has done a good job, then readers are often led to think that the writer is bursting to express genuine emotions ('feelings in search of a form') when it may in fact be the other way round ('form in search of a feeling') as the artist, working with a form (such as a sonnet), or a particular metre, will find that feelings emerge and colour his work with emotion which is itself freely invented. Writers have (after all) to write about something, and there is always the strong possibility that writers produce what the public will enjoy rather than what they are burning personally to impart. This argument is furthered by the fact that Juvenal exaggerates wildly and risks any personal credibility by his hyperbole. Orators in the 'real world' have to be plausible, but satire does not: it distorts and exaggerates the picture to the point where it can lose touch with real life for the sake of the entertainment being created. It looks 'staged' rather than heart-felt.

This could be used to get the poet off the hook in the eyes of many modern readers. *Satire* 6, for example, is a sustained attack on marriage. It purports to give advice to a certain Postumus to avoid getting married as all the different sorts of potential wives are hideous. The poet runs through the different ways in which women misbehave and creates vividly offensive caricatures of women to put Postumus off all of them. This sort of attitude is not without parallel in the ancient world but it is still pretty strong stuff and it is a difficult poem to read today without feeling revulsion. If, however, one were to see it as ironic mockery of misogyny itself rather than the real thing — assuming that the poet, in other words, adopts a 'mask' (*persona*) of 'woman-hater' and then writes a poem which such a man would deliver — then the purpose of the poem becomes the very opposite of what it appears to be. Far from espousing these revolting ideas, Juvenal is exposing these thoughts to ridicule as they are obviously idiotic. The 'indignation' which 'drives' him to verse (1.79) and which makes it difficult *not* to write satire (1.30) is itself perhaps a pose to lure the reader in, and the enraged old-testament prophet is in fact enjoying working his audience with the power of his rhetoric and his poetic skill, where the audience may choose to laugh either *with* or *at* the speaker so long as they enjoy the poem.

There is much to be said for this. Juvenal is writing in a world which enjoyed 'epideictic' oratory (where the point was to demonstrate oratorical subtlety rather than to prove a specific case) and with the memory of his own rhetorical training as a composer of *suasoriae* or 'set-piece speeches' such as he mocks in 1.17–18 and again in 7.161–4.

This was still very much in vogue in the oratorical and intellectual world of the 'Second Sophistic' in which Juvenal lived, and he was clearly a man of his times.

This is not, however, the end of the matter. The *persona* which the poet adopts may not be co-extensive with the poet himself, but it is the poet who chooses which *persona* to adopt and there is still scope for reading the text as in some ways revelatory of the mind of the writer and his age – if only to show what Romans would find interesting. Many of his less contentious arguments are over-stated but still resonate with us today and continue to haunt our thinking – what is worth dying (or killing) for? Is there any point in seeking to be rich? How should parents educate their children? How should we live our lives? – while others let us glimpse a world in which social values of 'nobility' and masculinity are questioned and discussed in language which is unparalleled for its frankness and power to make us think.

Readers must simply read the poems and decide the extent to which they are tongue-in-cheek or hand-on-heart, whether they are ironic rhetoric or examples of genuine emotion captured in expressive language. There is, after all, no one 'correct' way to read a poem. Roman literature was created with generic and metrical propriety, such that epic was always in hexameters and generally avoided vulgarities, while love-poetry tended to be in elegiac couplets and certain stock figures recur: but there is also a marked resistance to this restraint on the part of many writers who wish to avoid the tedium of predictability and seek to foil the expectations of their audience. Juvenal obviously wrote within the tradition of verse satire, but beyond that he resists categorization. The one thing we can say about him with confidence is that he was dedicated to being appreciated as a writer, and he uses the many skills of his trade to keep the readers on their toes and to surprise us with his skill. When he makes points which are facetious or plain wrong (and his blanket generalizations about women will fall into that category for many readers), then we end up admiring the style despite its content, and it is then that the mask slips to reveal the grinning ironist behind the text. In *Satire* 3, for instance, Umbricius claims to be fleeing from Greeks and vice which are everywhere in Rome, but also tells us that he is going to Cumae – a place which was full of both Greeks and vice, thus undermining his speech almost from the word go. Even if (as the poet's argument sometimes persuades us) all around is bad, mad, and sad, we are left with the poetry itself in which the views are so vividly and eloquently expressed.

A glossary of some literary terms

adynaton Statement of the impossible: e.g. 6.41–2.

alliteration Repetition of consonants: e.g. 6.111, 14.99, 15.60.

anaphora Repetition of the same word with insistent force in successive phrases: e.g. 6.29, 6.275–6, 14.111–12.

apostrophe Direct address to a character who is not present to the text: e.g. 6.80, 15.85.

assonance Repetition of vowel sounds: e.g. 14.77 (*vultur ium-*), 15.75 (*praestant instantibus*).

asyndeton Omission of connective words such as 'and': e.g. 6.353, 14.24.

bathos The effect achieved where 'high' language gives way to brutal and crude terms: e.g. 6.87, 14.91, 15.66.

bucolic diairesis Pause between the fourth and fifth foot of a hexameter: e.g. 14.114.

chiasmus Phrasing in which the second half reverses the word-order of the first (ABBA): e.g. 6.90, 14.12–13, 14.139, 15.71.

diatribe A verbal attack on a person or an idea.

diminutives A form of word which shows small size of (and/or affection for) a thing/person alluded to: e.g. 6.105, 14.138, 15.79.

ellipsis Omission of key word(s): e.g. 14.148.

enjambement Holding a final word of a phrase over the line-end to give it added emphasis at the start of the following line: e.g. 6.46, 14.13–14.

epanalepsis Repetition of a word from one line at the start of the next line: e.g. 6.34–5, 6.352–3.

epic language Words evocative of the style of epic poetry: e.g. 15.65–7.

focalization Seeing the events described through the senses of the person engaged in the action: e.g. 6.247, 14.190, 15.47.

gnomic statement Generalized universal statement: e.g. 6.361 *expavere.*

golden line A line which has two adjectives and two nouns framing a central verb (aaVnn): the first adjective agrees with the first noun, the second adjective with the second noun: e.g. 6.78, 15.46.

hendiadys Expressing a single concept with two nouns: e.g. 6.84.

hiatus Where a word ending with a vowel is followed by a word beginning with a vowel the two vowels usually elide into one sound: in hiatus both vowels are sounded separately: e.g. 6.274.

hyperbaton Unorthodox word order where a word is placed at a distance from other words with which it is to be taken: e.g. 6.355, 14.187–8, 15.63.

hyperbole Exaggeration: e.g. 6.9, 6.107–9, 6.410–11, 14.12, 15.61.

irony Affecting a tone of voice to alert the reader to the falseness of the words expressed: e.g. 6.1, 6.81, 14.23, 15.61.

juxtaposition Putting words next to each other for effects such as contrast or corroboration: e.g. 6.242, 14.80, 15.36.

litotes Understatement, such as 'not small' to mean 'large' (14.93).

metaphor Describing a person/thing with the imagery proper to something else: e.g. 6.95, 14.8, 15.35.

metonymy A word or name associated with something being used for the thing itself: e.g. 6.300, 15.29.

monosyllable A word of one syllable: e.g. 6.32, 14.92, 15.62.

onomatopoeia Choice of a word whose sound suggests its meaning: e.g. 14.5, 15.83.

oxymoron Juxtaposition of words with strongly contrasting meaning: e.g. 6.269, 14.2.

periphrasis Circumlocution – an indirect way of referring to someone/something: e.g. 6.40.

persona The 'mask' in the theatre: used of the character which the speaker of satire assumes when in his role as satirist.

pleonasm Saying more than is needed: e.g. 6.250, 14.31.

polyptoton The repetition of a word in different forms or cases: e.g. 6.28–9, 14.177–8.

polysyndeton Excessive use of connective words such as 'and' (the opposite of asyndeton): e.g. 14.219, 14.222.

rhetorical question Posing a question without expecting a reply: e.g. 6.252–3, 266–7, 14.177–8.

sarcasm Saying something in such a way as to suggest the opposite meaning: e.g. 6.38, 14.156–60, 15.84.

sibilance Use of the letter 's' for expressive effect: e.g. 15.80.

significant names Names which have a meaning which is relevant to the character of the person named: e.g. Fuscinus ('Mr Shady') in *Satire* 14.

spondaic rhythm A preponderance of heavy syllables: e.g. 6.80, 6.246, 14.19, 14.91, 15.36.

syncopation Rhythm where stresses fall on syllables other than the ones expected, often at the end of a line: e.g. 6.59, 14.101, 15.40.

synecdoche A form of metonymy in which a word denoting an aspect or part of something stands for the whole thing: e.g. 6.22, 14.162.

transferred epithet Applying a term which really describes one thing as part of the description of another thing: e.g. 6.31, 14.148, 15.43.

tricolon crescendo A rising pattern of three phrases, each one longer than the previous one: e.g. 6.28–9, 15.47–8.

The metre

Latin poetry was written in a fairly rigid system of metres, all of which in turn relied on the 'weight' of each syllable as either 'heavy' or 'light'.

Syllables are light (marked ∪ in this book) if the vowel is short and not followed by two (or more) consonants, whereas syllables containing long vowels, or diphthongs, or in which a vowel is followed by a succession of consonants, are heavy (–). A syllable is reckoned to be a single vowel sound, followed either by nothing (an 'open' syllable) or by a consonant (a 'closed' syllable): usually a single consonant following a vowel is reckoned to be the first consonant of the following syllable (e.g. *ca-li-gi-ne*) and does not affect the weight of the syllable. Where two or more consonants follow a vowel, the first one is included in the first syllable (*men-sa*) which is thus 'closed' and becomes heavy – the exceptions being combinations of mute and liquid consonants (*b, c, g, p, t* followed by *r*: and *c, p, t,* followed by *l*) where both letters are considered as belonging to the following syllable (*ma-tris*) and need not affect the rhythm of the line. Diphthongs (double vowels pronounced as a single sound such as *ae, eu, au*) are always long by nature: single vowels can in many cases change their quantity in different forms of a word: the final *-a* of *mensa* is long in the ablative case, short in the nominative, and the perfect tense of the verb *vĕnio* is *vēni*, for instance. This needs to be considered before any judgement is made about assonance – if the vowels have different quantities then there cannot be assonance and the only way to be sure is to scan the line.

In cases where a word ending with a vowel (or a vowel + *m* such as *iustam*) is followed by a word beginning with a vowel or *h*, the two syllables usually merge ('elide') into a single syllable, as at 14.110 where *triste habitu vultuque et* (nine syllables) is scanned *trist' habitu vultuqu' et* (seven syllables). There are also cases where the poet does not elide but leaves the gap ('hiatus') between the vowels, as at 6.274 (*sua atque*).

- – means a heavy syllable
- ∪ means a light syllable
- × means a syllable which may be either heavy or light
- // means the caesura (word-end in the middle of a foot of a hexameter).

The **hexameter** is the 'epic' metre used by Homer and all later epic and didactic poets: it also became (from Lucilius onwards) the metre of verse satire. The line is divided into six 'feet', each of which is either a dactyl (a heavy syllable followed by two light syllables (–∪∪ in conventional notation)) or a spondee (two heavy syllables (– –)). The last foot is always dissyllabic, and the last syllable of all may be either heavy or light. The metrical analysis of a line is called 'scansion' and a typical hexameter line (6.398) may be scanned thus:

– –/–∪∪/ –// –/ – –/ –∪∪/– –
sed can/tet poti/us// quam/ totam/ pervolet/ Urbem

where the // sign shows the 'caesura' – the word-break in the middle of a foot – which occurs in the third foot (as here) or in the fourth.

Latin also had a stress accent, whereby most words of more than one syllable were stressed on the penultimate syllable, or on the antepenultimate if the penultimate contained a short vowel. Thus, the second line of *Satire* 6 would be spoken:

in terris visamque diu cum frigida parvas

but 'scanned' metrically as:

in ter/ris vi/samque di/u cum/ frigida/ parvas

Here we can see that the metrical beat or 'ictus' clashes with the speech 'accent' in the first four feet and only coincides with it in the final two feet. This is common in all hexameter verse: occasionally poets avoid coincidence of ictus and accent in the final two feet as at 6.32, where the metrical ictus falls thus:

cum tibi/ vicin/um se/ praebeat/ Aemili/us pons

but the line is spoken thus:

cum tibi vicinum se praebeat Aemilius pons

Abbreviations

AG   Allen and Greenough *New Latin Grammar* (New York, Dover 2006)

CAH   *The Cambridge Ancient History*

OLD   *The Oxford Latin Dictionary*

OCD   *The Oxford Classical Dictionary*

Further reading

Editions of Juvenal include

Braund, S. M. *Juvenal Satires Book I* (text and commentary: Cambridge 1996).

Braund, S. M. *Juvenal and Persius* (Latin text with facing translation: Harvard University Press (Loeb Classical Library), 2004).

Clausen, W. V. *A. Persi Flacci et D. Iuni Iuvenalis Saturae* (Latin text: Oxford Classical Text 1992).

Courtney, E. *A Commentary on the Satires of Juvenal* (no text: California 1980, reprinted 2013).

Duff, J. D. *Juvenal Satires* (text and commentary: Cambridge, reprinted 1975).

Ferguson, J. *Juvenal the Satires* (text and commentary: London 1979).

Godwin, J. *Juvenal Satires Book III* (*Satires* 7–9: text with translation and commentary: Liverpool 2022).

Godwin, J. *Juvenal Satires Book IV* (*Satires* 10–12: text with translation and commentary: Liverpool 2016).

Godwin, J. *Juvenal Satires Book V* (*Satires* 13–16: text with translation and commentary: Liverpool 2020).

Hardy, E. G. *The Satires of Juvenal* (text and commentary: London 1963).

Housman, A. E. *D. Iunii Iuvenalis Saturae* (Cambridge 1931).

Mayor, J. E. B. *Thirteen Satires of Juvenal* (London 1886–9).

Ramsay, G. G. *Juvenal and Persius* (text and facing translation (Loeb Classical Library): London 1918).

Watson, L. and Watson, P. *Juvenal Satire 6* (text and commentary: Cambridge 2014).

Translations of Juvenal in English include

Green, P. *Juvenal: the Sixteen Satires* (Penguin Classics, revised edition 1998).

Rudd, N. *Juvenal: the Satires* (Oxford World's Classics 2008).

Books on Roman satire include

Braund, S. H. *Satire and Society in Ancient Rome* (Exeter 1989).

Braund, S. M. *The Roman Satirists and their Masks* (Bristol 2013).

Coffey, M. *Roman Satire* (London 1976).

Ferris-Hill, J. L. *Roman Satire and the Old Comic Tradition* (Cambridge 2015).

Freudenburg, K. *Satires of Rome* (Oxford 2001).

Freudenburg, K. *The Cambridge Companion to Roman Satire* (Cambridge 2005).

Hooley, D. *Roman Satire* (Oxford 2007).

Plaza, M. *The Function of Humour in Roman Verse Satire* (Oxford 2006).

Rosen, R. M. *Making Mockery: The Poetics of Ancient Satire* (Oxford 2007).

Rudd, N. *Themes in Roman Satire* (Bristol 1998).

Sullivan, J. P. (ed.). *Critical Essays on Roman Literature: Satire* (London 1963).

Critical books on Juvenal include

Geue, T. *Juvenal and the Poetics of Anonymity* (Cambridge 2017).

Highet, G. *Juvenal the Satirist* (Oxford 1954).

Jenkyns, R. *Three Classical Poets: Sappho, Catullus and Juvenal* (London 1982).

Jones, F. M. A. *Juvenal and the Satiric Genre* (London 2007).

Keane, C. *Juvenal and the Satiric Emotions* (Oxford 2015).

Uden, J. *The Invisible Satirist: Juvenal and Second-Century Rome* (Oxford 2015).

Useful collections of articles on Juvenal include

Braund, S. and J. Osgood (eds). *A Companion to Persius and Juvenal* (Oxford 2012).

Plaza, M. (ed.). *Persius and Juvenal* (a collection of important articles: Oxford Readings in Classical Studies 2009).

On *Satire* 6 and Roman women see also

Balsdon, J. P. V. D. *Roman Women: Their History and Habits* (London 1962).

Braund, S. M. 'Juvenal – misogynist or misogamist?' *Journal of Roman Studies* 82 (1992): 71–86.

Dixon, S. *Reading Roman Women* (London 2001).

Gold, B. K. '"The house I live in is not my own": Women's Bodies in Juvenal's Satires', *Arethusa* 31 (1998): 369–86.

Pomeroy, S. *Goddesses, Whores, Wives and Slaves* (London 1994).

Sulprizio, C. *Gender and Sexuality in Juvenal's Rome* (modern translation (with notes) of *Satires* 2 and 6: Oklahoma 2021).

On Juvenal's sexual terminology see

Adams, J. N. *The Latin Sexual Vocabulary* (London 1982).

On Roman marriage see

Treggiari, S. *Roman Marriage* (Oxford 1991).

On *Satire* 14 see also

Corn, A. 'Thus Nature Ordains: Juvenal's Fourtneeth Satire', *Illinois Classical Studies* 17 (1992): 309–22.

O'Neill, E. N. 'The Structure of Juvenal's Fourteenth Satire', *Classical Philology* 55 (1960): 251–3.

Stein, J. P. 'The Unity and Scope of Juvenal's Fourteenth Satire', *Classical Philology* 65 (1970): 34–6.

On *Satire* 15 see also

Anderson, W. S. 'Cannibals and Culture', *Ramus* 16 (1987): 203–14.

McKim, R. 'Philosophers and Cannibals: Juvenal's Fifteenth Satire', *Phoenix* 40 (1986): 58–71.

Powell, B. B. 'What Juvenal saw: Egyptian Religion and Anthropophagy in
    Satire 15', *Rheinisches Museum* 122 (1979): 185–9.
Singleton, D. 'Juvenal's Fifteenth Satire: A Reading', *Greece & Rome*, Vol. 30,
    No. 2 (1983): 198–207.

On the use of metre see

Morgan, L. *Musa Pedestris – Metre and Meaning in Roman Verse* (Oxford
    2010).
Raven, D. S. *Latin Metre* (new edition: London 2010).

Text

6

credo Pudicitiam Saturno rege moratam
in terris visamque diu, cum frigida parvas
praeberet spelunca domos ignemque laremque
et pecus et dominos communi clauderet umbra,
silvestrem montana torum cum sterneret uxor   5
frondibus et culmo vicinarumque ferarum
pellibus, haud similis tibi, Cynthia, nec tibi, cuius
turbavit nitidos exstinctus passer ocellos,
sed potanda ferens infantibus ubera magnis
et saepe horridior glandem ructante marito.   10
quippe aliter tunc orbe novo caeloque recenti
vivebant homines, qui rupto robore nati
compositive luto nullos habuere parentes.
multa Pudicitiae veteris vestigia forsan
aut aliqua exstiterint et sub Iove, sed Iove nondum   15
barbato, nondum Graecis iurare paratis
per caput alterius, cum furem nemo timeret
caulibus ac pomis et aperto viveret horto.
paulatim deinde ad superos Astraea recessit
hac comite, atque duae pariter fugere sorores.   20
anticum et vetus est alienum, Postume, lectum
concutere atque sacri genium contemnere fulcri.
omne aliud crimen mox ferrea protulit aetas:
viderunt primos argentea saecula moechos.
conventum tamen et pactum et sponsalia nostra   25
tempestate paras iamque a tonsore magistro
pecteris et digito pignus fortasse dedisti?
certe sanus eras. uxorem, Postume, ducis?

dic qua Tisiphone, quibus exagitere colubris.
ferre potes dominam salvis tot restibus ullam, 30
cum pateant altae caligantesque fenestrae,
cum tibi vicinum se praebeat Aemilius pons?
aut si de multis nullus placet exitus, illud
nonne putas melius, quod tecum pusio dormit -
pusio, qui noctu non litigat, exigit a te 35
nulla iacens illic munuscula, nec queritur quod
et lateri parcas nec quantum iussit anheles?
sed placet Ursidio lex Iulia: tollere dulcem
cogitat heredem, cariturus turture magno
mullorumque iubis et captatore macello. 40
quid fieri non posse putes, si iungitur ulla
Ursidio? si moechorum notissimus olim
stulta maritali iam porrigit ora capistro,
quem totiens texit perituri cista Latini?
quid quod et antiquis uxor de moribus illi 45
quaeritur? o medici, nimiam pertundite venam.
delicias hominis! Tarpeium limen adora
pronus et auratam Iunoni caede iuvencam,
si tibi contigerit capitis matrona pudici.
paucae adeo Cereris vittas contingere dignae, 50
quarum non timeat pater oscula. necte coronam
postibus et densos per limina tende corymbos!
unus Hiberinae vir sufficit? ocius illud
extorquebis, ut haec oculo contenta sit uno.
'magna tamen fama est cuiusdam rure paterno 55
viventis'. vivat Gabiis ut vixit in agro,
vivat Fidenis, et 'agello' cedo 'paterno'.
quis tamen affirmat nil actum in montibus aut in
speluncis? adeo senuerunt Iuppiter et Mars?
porticibusne tibi monstratur femina voto 60
digna tuo? cuneis an habent spectacula totis
quod securus ames quodque inde excerpere possis?
chironomon Ledam molli saltante Bathyllo

Tuccia vesicae non imperat, Apula gannit,
sicut in amplexu, subito et miserabile longum. 65
attendit Thymele: Thymele tunc rustica discit.
ast aliae, quotiens aulaea recondita cessant,
et vacuo clausoque sonant fora sola theatro,
atque a Plebeis longe Megalesia, tristes
personam thyrsumque tenent et subligar Acci. 70
Urbicus exodio risum movet Atellanae
gestibus Autonoes, hunc diligit Aelia pauper.
solvitur his magno comoedi fibula, sunt quae
Chrysogonum cantare vetent, Hispulla tragoedo
gaudet: an expectas ut Quintilianus ametur? 75
accipis uxorem de qua citharoedus Echion
aut Glaphyrus fiat pater Ambrosiusque choraules.
longa per angustos figamus pulpita vicos,
ornentur postes et grandi ianua lauro,
ut testudineo tibi, Lentule, conopeo 80
nobilis Euryalum murmillonem exprimat infans.
nupta senatori comitata est Eppia ludum
ad Pharon et Nilum famosaque moenia Lagi,
prodigia et mores Urbis damnante Canopo.
immemor illa domus et coniugis atque sororis 85
nil patriae indulsit, plorantesque improba natos -
utque magis stupeas – ludos Paridemque reliquit.
sed quamquam in magnis opibus plumaque paterna
et segmentatis dormisset parvula cunis,
contempsit pelagus; famam contempserat olim, 90
cuius apud molles minima est iactura cathedras.
Tyrrhenos igitur fluctus lateque sonantem
pertulit Ionium constanti pectore, quamvis
mutandum totiens esset mare. iusta pericli
si ratio est et honesta, timent pavidoque gelantur 95
pectore nec tremulis possunt insistere plantis:
fortem animum praestant rebus quas turpiter audent.
si iubeat coniunx, durum est conscendere navem,

tunc sentina gravis, tunc summus vertitur aer:
quae moechum sequitur, stomacho valet. illa maritum   100
convomit, haec inter nautas et prandet et errat
per puppem et duros gaudet tractare rudentes.
qua tamen exarsit forma, qua capta iuventa
Eppia? quid vidit propter quod ludia dici
sustinuit? nam Sergiolus iam radere guttur   105
coeperat et secto requiem sperare lacerto;
praeterea multa in facie deformia: sulcus
attritus galea mediisque in naribus ingens
gibbus et acre malum semper stillantis ocelli.
sed gladiator erat. facit hoc illos Hyacinthos: 110
hoc pueris patriaeque, hoc praetulit illa sorori
atque viro. ferrum est quod amant. hic Sergius idem
accepta rude coepisset Veiiento videri.

*114–241: Such scandals even happened in the emperor's own palace in
the case of Messalina. Women will do anything to satisfy their lust and
supposedly happy husbands must have their own ulterior motives (such
as money or sex) for staying married – and good women are intolerably
proud anyway. Some women are mad on all things Greek: and don't get
married unless you want to be treated like a slave in your own home.
Their mothers also connive at their infidelity.*

nulla fere causa est in qua non femina litem
moverit. accusat Manilia, si rea non est.
componunt ipsae per se formantque libellos,
principium atque locos Celso dictare paratae.   245
endromidas Tyrias et femineum ceroma
quis nescit, vel quis non vidit vulnera pali,
quem cavat assiduis rudibus scutoque lacessit
atque omnes implet numeros dignissima prorsus
Florali matrona tuba, nisi si quid in illo   250
pectore plus agitat veraeque paratur harenae?
quem praestare potest mulier galeata pudorem,

quae fugit a sexu? vires amat. haec tamen ipsa
vir nollet fieri; nam quantula nostra voluptas!
quale decus, rerum si coniugis auctio fiat,   255
balteus et manicae et cristae crurisque sinistri
dimidium tegimen! vel si diversa movebit
proelia, tu felix ocreas vendente puella.
hae sunt quae tenui sudant in cyclade, quarum
delicias et panniculus bombycinus urit.   260
aspice quo fremitu monstratos perferat ictus
et quanto galeae curvetur pondere, quanta
poplitibus sedeat quam denso fascia libro,
et ride positis scaphium cum sumitur armis.
dicite vos, neptes Lepidi caecive Metelli   265
Gurgitis aut Fabii, quae ludia sumpserit umquam
hos habitus? quando ad palum gemat uxor Asyli?
semper habet lites alternaque iurgia lectus
in quo nupta iacet; minimum dormitur in illo.
tum gravis illa viro, tunc orba tigride peior,   270
cum simulat gemitus occulti conscia facti.
aut odit pueros aut ficta paelice plorat
uberibus semper lacrimis semperque paratis
in statione sua atque expectantibus illam,
quo iubeat manare modo. tu credis amorem,   275
tu tibi tunc, uruca, places fletumque labellis
exsorbes, quae scripta et quot lecture tabellas
si tibi zelotypae retegantur scrinia moechae!
sed iacet in servi complexibus aut equitis. 'dic,
dic aliquem sodes hic, Quintiliane, colorem.'   280
'haeremus. dic ipsa.' 'olim convenerat' inquit
'ut faceres tu quod velles, nec non ego possem
indulgere mihi. clames licet et mare caelo
confundas, homo sum.' nihil est audacius illis
deprensis: iram atque animos a crimine sumunt.   285
unde haec monstra tamen vel quo de fonte requiris?
praestabat castas humilis fortuna Latinas

quondam, nec vitiis contingi parva sinebant
tecta labor somnique breves et vellere Tusco
vexatae duraeque manus ac proximus Urbi   290
Hannibal et stantes Collina turre mariti.
nunc patimur longae pacis mala, saevior armis
luxuria incubuit victumque ulciscitur orbem.
nullum crimen abest facinusque libidinis ex quo
paupertas Romana perit. hinc fluxit ad istos   295
et Sybaris colles, hinc et Rhodos et Miletos
atque coronatum et petulans madidumque Tarentum.
prima peregrinos obscena pecunia mores
intulit, et turpi fregerunt saecula luxu
divitiae molles. quid enim Venus ebria curat?   300
inguinis et capitis quae sint discrimina nescit,
grandia quae mediis iam noctibus ostrea mordet,
cum perfusa mero spumant unguenta Falerno,
cum bibitur concha, cum iam vertigine tectum
ambulat et geminis exsurgit mensa lucernis.   305

306–51: The speaker describes the rites of the Bona Dea, where women go mad in an orgy of drunken lust. Women of all classes are equally debauched.

ut spectet ludos, conducit Ogulnia vestem,
conducit comites, sellam, cervical, amicas,
nutricem et flavam cui det mandata puellam.
haec tamen argenti superest quodcumque paterni   355
levibus athletis et vasa novissima donat.
multis res angusta domi, sed nulla pudorem
paupertatis habet nec se metitur ad illum
quem dedit haec posuitque modum. tamen utile quid sit
prospiciunt aliquando viri, frigusque famemque   360
formica tandem quidam expavere magistra:
prodiga non sentit pereuntem femina censum.
ac velut exhausta recidivus pullulet arca
nummus et e pleno tollatur semper acervo,
non umquam reputant quanti sibi gaudia constent.   365

*366–97: Women bring into the house a motley crowd of people: perverts,
eunuchs and musicians.*

sed cantet potius quam totam pervolet Urbem
audax et coetus possit quae ferre virorum
cumque paludatis ducibus praesente marito   400
ipsa loqui recta facie siccisque mamillis.
haec eadem novit quid toto fiat in orbe,
quid Seres, quid Thraces agant, secreta novercae
et pueri, quis amet, quis diripiatur adulter;
dicet quis viduam praegnatem fecerit et quo   405
mense, quibus verbis concumbat quaeque, modis quot.
instantem regi Armenio Parthoque cometen
prima videt, famam rumoresque illa recentes
excipit ad portas, quosdam facit; isse Niphaten
in populos magnoque illic cuncta arva teneri   410
diluvio, nutare urbes, subsidere terras,
quocumque in trivio, cuicumque est obvia, narrat.

*The rest of the poem describes other sorts of women: the angry wife, the
argumentative wife, the wives who love jewellery too much or are cruel
to their slaves, the superstitious wives who employ fake fortune-tellers,
the ones who procure abortions or else import into the house other
people's babies as their own, and wives who harm their husbands with
love-potions. The poem ends with murderous wives who murder their
children and their husbands.*

AS

14

plurima sunt, Fuscine, et fama digna sinistra
et nitidis maculam haesuram figentia rebus,
quae monstrant ipsi pueris traduntque parentes.
si damnosa senem iuvat alea, ludit et heres
bullatus parvoque eadem movet arma fritillo.   5
nec melius de se cuiquam sperare propinquo
concedet iuvenis, qui radere tubera terrae,
boletum condire et eodem iure natantes
mergere ficedulas didicit nebulone parente
et cana monstrante gula. cum septimus annus   10
transierit puerum, nondum omni dente renato,
barbatos licet admoveas mille inde magistros,
hinc totidem, cupiet lauto cenare paratu
semper et a magna non degenerare culina.
quid suadet iuveni laetus stridore catenae,   23
quem mire afficiunt inscripta, ergastula, carcer?   24
mitem animum et mores modicis erroribus aequos   15
praecipit utque animas servorum et corpora nostra
materia constare putet paribusque elementis,
an saevire docet Rutilus, qui gaudet acerbo
plagarum strepitu et nullam Sirena flagellis
comparat, Antiphates trepidi laris ac Polyphemus,   20
tunc felix, quotiens aliquis tortore vocato
uritur ardenti duo propter lintea ferro?
rusticus expectas ut non sit adultera Largae   25
filia, quae numquam maternos dicere moechos
tam cito nec tanto poterit contexere cursu
ut non ter deciens respiret? conscia matri
virgo fuit; ceras nunc hac dictante pusillas
implet et ad moechum dat eisdem ferre cinaedis.   30
sic natura iubet: velocius et citius nos
corrumpunt vitiorum exempla domestica, magnis
cum subeant animos auctoribus.

**A
Level**

34–73: We can all be taught bad ways and children should be protected from bad behaviour and bad language. How can you later reprimand a son who is only copying your bad behaviour? You make more effort to clean your house for visitors than to clean your life for your children.

serpente ciconia pullos
nutrit et inventa per devia rura lacerta: 75
illi eadem sumptis quaerunt animalia pinnis.
vultur iumento et canibus crucibusque relictis
ad fetus properat partemque cadaveris affert:
hic est ergo cibus magni quoque vulturis et se
pascentis, propria cum iam facit arbore nidos.   80
sed leporem aut capream famulae Iovis et generosae
in saltu venantur aves, hinc praeda cubili
ponitur: inde autem cum se matura levavit
progenies stimulante fame festinat ad illam
quam primum praedam rupto gustaverat ovo.   85
aedificator erat Caetronius et modo curvo
litore Caietae, summa nunc Tiburis arce,
nunc Praenestinis in montibus alta parabat
culmina villarum Graecis longeque petitis
marmoribus vincens Fortunae atque Herculis aedem,   90
ut spado vincebat Capitolia nostra Posides.
dum sic ergo habitat Caetronius, imminuit rem,
fregit opes, nec parva tamen mensura relictae
partis erat. totam hanc turbavit filius amens,
dum meliore novas attollit marmore villas.   95
quidam sortiti metuentem sabbata patrem
nil praeter nubes et caeli numen adorant,
nec distare putant humana carne suillam,
qua pater abstinuit, mox et praeputia ponunt;
Romanas autem soliti contemnere leges   100
Iudaicum ediscunt et servant ac metuunt ius,
tradidit arcano quodcumque volumine Moyses:
non monstrare vias eadem nisi sacra colenti,

**A
Level**

quaesitum ad fontem solos deducere verpos.
sed pater in causa, cui septima quaeque fuit lux   105
ignava et partem vitae non attigit ullam.
sponte tamen iuvenes imitantur cetera, solam
inviti quoque avaritiam exercere iubentur.
fallit enim vitium specie virtutis et umbra,
cum sit triste habitu vultuque et veste severum,   110
nec dubie tamquam frugi laudetur avarus,
tamquam parcus homo et rerum tutela suarum
certa magis quam si fortunas servet easdem
Hesperidum serpens aut Ponticus. adde quod hunc de
quo loquor egregium populus putat acquirendi   115
artificem; quippe his crescunt patrimonia fabris
sed crescunt quocumque modo. maioraque fiunt
incude assidua semperque ardente camino.
et pater ergo animi felices credit avaros
qui miratur opes, qui nulla exempla beati   120
pauperis esse putat, iuvenes hortatur ut illa
ire via pergant et eidem incumbere sectae.
sunt quaedam vitiorum elementa, his protinus illos
imbuit et cogit minimas ediscere sordes;
mox acquirendi docet insatiabile votum.   125
servorum ventres modio castigat iniquo
ipse quoque esuriens, neque enim omnia sustinet umquam
mucida caerulei panis consumere frusta,
hesternum solitus medio servare minutal
Septembri nec non differre in tempora cenae   130
alterius conchem aestivam cum parte lacerti
signatam vel dimidio putrique siluro
filaque sectivi numerata includere porri.
invitatus ad haec aliquis de ponte negabit.
sed quo divitias haec per tormenta coactas,   135
cum furor haud dubius, cum sit manifesta phrenesis,
ut locuples moriaris, egentis vivere fato?
interea, pleno cum turget sacculus ore,

A
Level

crescit amor nummi quantum ipsa pecunia crevit,
et minus hanc optat qui non habet. ergo paratur 140
altera villa tibi, cum rus non sufficit unum
et proferre libet fines maiorque videtur
et melior vicina seges; mercaris et hanc et
arbusta et densa montem qui canet oliva.
quorum si pretio dominus non vincitur ullo, 145
nocte boves macri lassoque famelica collo
iumenta ad virides huius mittentur aristas
nec prius inde domum quam tota novalia saevos
in ventres abeant, ut credas falcibus actum.
dicere vix possis quam multi talia plorent 150
et quot venales iniuria fecerit agros.
sed qui sermones, quam foede bucina famae!
'quid nocet haec?' inquit 'tunicam mihi malo lupini
quam si me toto laudet vicinia pago
exigui ruris paucissima farra secantem.' 155
scilicet et morbis et debilitate carebis
et luctum et curam effugies, et tempora vitae
longa tibi posthac fato meliore dabuntur,
si tantum culti solus possederis agri
quantum sub Tatio populus Romanus arabat. 160
mox etiam fractis aetate ac Punica passis
proelia vel Pyrrhum immanem gladiosque Molossos
tandem pro multis vix iugera bina dabantur
vulneribus; merces haec sanguinis atque laboris
nulli visa umquam meritis minor aut ingratae 165
curta fides patriae. saturabat glebula talis
patrem ipsum turbamque casae, qua feta iacebat
uxor et infantes ludebant quattuor, unus
vernula, tres domini; sed magnis fratribus horum
a scrobe vel sulco redeuntibus altera cena 170
amplior et grandes fumabant pultibus ollae.
nunc modus hic agri nostro non sufficit horto.
inde fere scelerum causae, nec plura venena

miscuit aut ferro grassatur saepius ullum
humanae mentis vitium quam saeva cupido   175
immodici census. nam dives qui fieri vult,
et cito vult fieri; sed quae reverentia legum,
quis metus aut pudor est umquam properantis avari?
'vivite contenti casulis et collibus istis,
o pueri!' Marsus dicebat et Hernicus olim   180
Vestinusque senex, 'panem quaeramus aratro,
qui satis est mensis: laudant hoc numina ruris,
quorum ope et auxilio gratae post munus aristae
contingunt homini veteris fastidia quercus.
nil vetitum fecisse volet, quem non pudet alto   185
per glaciem perone tegi, qui summovet Euros
pellibus inversis: peregrina ignotaque nobis
ad scelus atque nefas, quaecumque est, purpura ducit.'
haec illi veteres praecepta minoribus; at nunc
post finem autumni media de nocte supinum   190
clamosus iuvenem pater excitat: 'accipe ceras,
scribe, puer, vigila, causas age, perlege rubras
maiorum leges; aut vitem posce libello,
sed caput intactum buxo naresque pilosas
adnotet et grandes miretur Laelius alas;   195
dirue Maurorum attegias, castella Brigantum,
ut locupletem aquilam tibi sexagesimus annus
afferat; aut, longos castrorum ferre labores
si piget et trepidum solvunt tibi cornua ventrem
cum lituis audita, pares quod vendere possis   200
pluris dimidio, nec te fastidia mercis
ullius subeant ablegandae Tiberim ultra,
neu credas ponendum aliquid discriminis inter
unguenta et corium: lucri bonus est odor ex re
qualibet. illa tuo sententia semper in ore   205
versetur dis atque ipso Iove digna poeta:
"unde habeas quaerit nemo, sed oportet habere."'

hoc monstrant vetulae pueris repentibus assae,
hoc discunt omnes ante alpha et beta puellae.
talibus instantem monitis quemcumque parentem   210
sic possem affari: 'dic, o vanissime, quis te
festinare iubet? meliorem praesto magistro
discipulum. securus abi: vinceris, ut Aiax
praeteriit Telamonem, ut Pelea vicit Achilles.
parcendum est teneris; nondum implevere medullas   215
maturae mala nequitiae. cum ponere barbam
coeperit et longi mucronem admittere cultri,
falsus erit testis, vendet periuria summa
exigua et Cereris tangens aramque pedemque.
elatam iam crede nurum, si limina vestra   220
mortifera cum dote subit. quibus illa premetur
per somnum digitis! nam quae terraque marique
acquirenda putas brevior via conferet illi;
nullus enim magni sceleris labor. "haec ego numquam
mandavi" dices olim "nec talia suasi."   225
mentis causa malae tamen est et origo penes te.
nam quisquis magni census praecepit amorem
et laevo monitu pueros producit avaros
quippe et per fraudes patrimonia conduplicari
dat libertatem et totas effundit habenas   230
curriculo; quem si revoces, subsistere nescit
et te contempto rapitur metisque relictis.

233–331: Parents need to beware of teaching their children to grow up rapacious and impatient to inherit the family estate by murder if necessary. People take huge risks to make money in trade and their antics are more outrageous than anything seen on the stage. If they make a fortune they can never relax for fear of being robbed. How much money does anyone need? Only enough to satisfy hunger, thirst and cold.

A Level

15

1–26: The Egyptians are a strange race. They worship animals as if they were gods but have no qualms about eating people. Ulysses' tales of cannibalism must have provoked angry disbelief among his Phaeacian audience but such things really happen in Egypt.

nos miranda quidem sed nuper consule Iunco
gesta super calidae referemus moenia Copti,
nos vulgi scelus et cunctis graviora cothurnis;
nam scelus, a Pyrrha quamquam omnia syrmata volvas,   30
nullus apud tragicos populus facit. accipe nostro
dira quod exemplum feritas produxerit aevo.
inter finitimos vetus atque antiqua simultas,
immortale odium et numquam sanabile vulnus,
ardet adhuc Ombos et Tentyra. summus utrimque   35
inde furor vulgo, quod numina vicinorum
odit uterque locus, cum solos credat habendos
esse deos quos ipse colit. sed tempore festo
alterius populi rapienda occasio cunctis
visa inimicorum primoribus ac ducibus, ne   40
laetum hilaremque diem, ne magnae gaudia cenae
sentirent positis ad templa et compita mensis
pervigilique toro, quem nocte ac luce iacentem
septimus interdum sol invenit. horrida sane
Aegyptus, sed luxuria, quantum ipse notavi,   45
barbara famoso non cedit turba Canopo.
adde quod et facilis victoria de madidis et
blaesis atque mero titubantibus. inde virorum
saltatus nigro tibicine, qualiacumque
unguenta et flores multaeque in fronte coronae: 50
hinc ieiunum odium. sed iurgia prima sonare
incipiunt; animis ardentibus haec tuba rixae.
dein clamore pari concurritur, et vice teli
saevit nuda manus. paucae sine vulnere malae,

vix cuiquam aut nulli toto certamine nasus 55
integer. aspiceres iam cuncta per agmina vultus
dimidios, alias facies et hiantia ruptis
ossa genis, plenos oculorum sanguine pugnos.
ludere se credunt ipsi tamen et pueriles
exercere acies quod nulla cadavera calcent. 60
et sane quo tot rixantis milia turbae,
si vivunt omnes? ergo acrior impetus et iam
saxa inclinatis per humum quaesita lacertis
incipiunt torquere, domestica seditioni
tela, nec hunc lapidem, quales et Turnus et Aiax, 65
vel quo Tydides percussit pondere coxam
Aeneae, sed quem valeant emittere dextrae
illis dissimiles et nostro tempore natae.
nam genus hoc vivo iam decrescebat Homero,
terra malos homines nunc educat atque pusillos; 70
ergo deus, quicumque aspexit, ridet et odit.
a deverticulo repetatur fabula. postquam
subsidiis aucti, pars altera promere ferrum
audet et infestis pugnam instaurare sagittis.
terga fugae celeri praestant instantibus Ombis 75
qui vicina colunt umbrosae Tentyra palmae.
labitur hic quidam nimia formidine cursum
praecipitans capiturque. ast illum in plurima sectum
frusta et particulas, ut multis mortuus unus
sufficeret, totum corrosis ossibus edit 80
victrix turba, nec ardenti decoxit aeno
aut veribus, longum usque adeo tardumque putavit
expectare focos, contenta cadavere crudo.
hic gaudere libet quod non violaverit ignem,
quem summa caeli raptum de parte, Prometheu, 85
donasti terris; elemento gratulor, et te
exultare reor. sed qui mordere cadaver
sustinuit nil umquam hac carne libentius edit;
nam scelere in tanto ne quaeras et dubites an

prima voluptatem gula senserit, ultimus ante   90
qui stetit, absumpto iam toto corpore ductis
per terram digitis aliquid de sanguine gustat.

*93–174: The speaker goes on to describe the cannibalism of the Vascones,
which was forced upon them by starvation and so was excusable (unlike
that of the Egyptians). He ends the poem more positively: humans must
show compassion towards each other, or they behave worse than wild
animals.*

Commentary Notes

Satire 6

This poem makes up the whole of Juvenal's second book of *Satires* and is the longest single verse satire to have survived from antiquity. It purports to be an attempt to persuade a certain Postumus not to get married (25–8): the 'evidence' adduced to support this case is a series of case-studies showing the appalling suffering which husbands undergo at the hands of their wives. Wives are described as being any or all of the following: incorrigibly randy, drunken, proud, quarrelsome, unfaithful, unfeminine, uncouth, too clever, superstitious, and liable to murder their menfolk. The poem ends with the vignette of mythical heroines working for real in Rome – 'every street will have its own Clytemnestra' (656) – alluding to the Greek queen who murdered her husband Agamemnon to be free to replace him with her lover.

1–24

Adultery has a long history: marital fidelity may have existed in the Golden Age of Saturn and even into the beginning of Jupiter's sovereignty, when theft was unknown, but it soon became common practice to commit adultery, and other crimes soon followed in the Iron Age.

The poem begins with a satirical account of primeval humanity living a simple life of moral virtue, arguing that we shed our morals along with our caveman lifestyle. Some of the ideas are reminiscent of earlier writings (see 'further notes' online) on the development of civilization, but these ideas are overlaid here with irony, as the poet gives us a withering demythologization of the moral paradise of the 'Golden

Age': primitive humans had nothing worth stealing and their wives were too ugly to attract lovers, which explains their 'virtue' as merely a necessary by-product of their harsh and crude lifestyle. Juvenal's cynical eye usually looks for an unflattering reason to account for apparently good behaviour and this opening paragraph is no exception.

1 The first word (**credo**) is ironic ('I believe' suggests 'though others do not') and the poet at once evokes the world of myth with the imagery of the goddess *Pudicitia* (Chastity) lingering on earth during the reign of Saturn (who was expelled from his throne by his son Jupiter) and then shortly afterwards leaving us. Saturn's reign was regarded by the Romans as a 'Golden Age' when humans lived in perfect peace and idyllic bliss. **pudicitia** is marital fidelity – a quality of paramount importance in a Roman wife and one which this poem will demand and desire throughout. *esse* needs to be understood with **moratam** to form the perfect infinitive of the deponent verb *moror*. **Saturno rege** is an ablative absolute (with implied participle from the verb 'to be'). The final vowel of **credŏ** is scanned short.

2 **visam** is significant, reminding us that in mythology gods and humans would see each other, until human wickedness forced us apart (cf. Catullus 64.384–408).

2-3 Early man is depicted as living a spartan life: a cold cave (**frigida ... spelunca**) provides only small (**parvas**) homes, with the typically Roman features of hearth (**ignem**) and household god (**larem**).

4 These humans kept their animals in the cave with them and the beasts (**pecus**) and their masters (**dominos**) are juxtaposed in the verse as in the cave. The final word **umbra** is an anticlimax: we expect something more positive to go with the word 'shared' (**communi**) than 'gloom': **communi** reminds us of the mutual support offered and enjoyed by early mankind (described in 15.148–58).

5–7 The primitive setting is stressed both by the juxtaposition of **silvestrem montana** (evoking the landscape of woods and mountain) and the description of the bivouac bedding made from leaves, straw and animal hides.

5 The first woman in the poem is in many ways a model wife – she is a chaste home-maker and a mother to sturdy infants – but the idyll is debunked in grim rustic terms: this is a 'mountain wife' (**montana uxor**), suggesting that she is a tough hillbilly.

6 The wild beasts (**ferarum**) are her 'neighbours' while the flock (**pecus**) are her housemates.

7–8 **Cynthia** was the name which the Roman love-poet Propertius gave to his mistress: she was known (Propertius 1.2.2, 2.1.6–7) for her wearing of alluring diaphanous 'Coan garments' and it is amusing to see her compared to this woman who is dressed in animal hides. Juvenal then addresses Catullus' mistress in the second person (**tibi**) with the device known as 'apostrophe' whereby the writer directly addresses an absent character, a trope familiar from Homer (*Iliad* 16.843, *Odyssey* 14.55) and used elsewhere by Juvenal (15.85). Catullus describes (2–3) how his mistress had a beloved pet sparrow whose death left her 'lovely little eyes' (*ocelli*) 'red and swollen with weeping' (3.18), in contrast to the cavewoman who brought about the death of animals to clothe herself. Juvenal clearly expects his readers to identify these love-poets without naming them.

9 The breastfeeding is written up in hyperbolic style. The children were big (**magnis**) in accordance with the common idea that primitive man was stronger and tougher than modern generations; the breasts are called 'udders' (**ubera**) (a term more appropriate to the herd than to humans), and they are so huge that the woman is 'carrying' them (**ferens**). Finally, the word *potare* is more commonly used of excessive drinking in adults and is comic when applied to a giant suckling infant.

10 The final line of this ten-line sentence is a masterstroke of satirical force: the woman is in many cases 'shaggier' (**horridior**) than her husband – and he is described with the powerful auditory (and olfactory) term 'acorn-belching'. When both sexes were as repellent as this, it is not surprising that people did not indulge in adultery. Acorns were supposedly a staple food of primitive man.

11 **quippe** has explanatory force ('the reason being that ... '). The youth of the world at that time is evoked with a double phrase, with variation of vocabulary (**novo ... recenti**) and parallel citing of earth (**orbe**) and sky (**caelo**).

12–13 Ancient societies asked themselves how the first humans came into being and theorized that the first men were born from living trees or out of the earth itself: one famous myth has the Titan Prometheus fashioning men out of mud (cf. 14.35). The simple image of men 'born from an oak-tree' (**robore nati**) is here animated with the powerful participle **rupto** suggestive of the tree splitting open and uncovering the new-born human.

13 Having no parents is inevitable in the first humans: here there is a moral jibe that parents usually corrupt their children (as stated throughout *Satire* 14) and so people would be more virtuous when born from trees and mud than when born from Romans. **habuere** is the alternative form of *habuerunt* (third person plural of the perfect of *habeo*).

14–15 After the expulsion of Saturn came the reign of Jupiter when mankind's behaviour deteriorated: the speaker speculates (**forsan**) that 'many' (**multa**) traces of chastity, or at least 'some' (**aliqua**) continued to exist 'even (**et**) under Jupiter' – but only while Jupiter was a young god.

15–16 **barbato** literally means 'bearded': Jupiter was a notorious adulterer and this comic image of the beardless god hints that women were only safe until he grew his beard.

AS

16–18 The crimes mentioned here are perjury and theft rather than sexual crime, but Romans regarded adultery as a form of theft (cf. 6. O32, Catullus 7.8, 68.140) and the breaking of a marriage oath through adultery was also a form of perjury.

16–17 Juvenal was a harsh (and unfair) critic of Greeks (see 3.58– 125) and regarded them both as habitual liars and also sexually voracious (cf. 3.109–12). For someone to swear an oath on their own life – and so invite misfortune if the oath was a lie – was one thing: Greeks would swear falsely on somebody else's (**alterius**) head and leave them to incur the misfortune, combining perjury with potential harm. The phrase **Graecis ... paratis** is an ablative absolute construction parallel to the previous ablative absolute **Iove ... barbato**.

17–18 The speaker first mentions the thief (**furem**) and only then specifies the goods threatened by him – the anticlimactic 'cabbages and apples'. The speaker reminds us that this is a rural setting and (as with the married couple in 5–10) suggests that nobody stole because there was little worth stealing. **caulibus ac pomis** is dative case going with **timeret** ('feared for his cabbages and apples') and **furem** ('thief') indicates the precise threat (not) facing them. The subject of **viveret** is a generalized 'one' drawn from **nemo** in the line above.

19–20 These two lines recall the opening of the poem, with **hac** referring to **Pudicitia** in line 1 and **paulatim** recalling **moratam**. **Astraea** was the divine embodiment of Justice. **fugēre** is the third person plural of the perfect tense of *fugio*.

21 *anticus* is the archaic form of *antiquus* and the archaism reinforces the 'antiquity' being pointed out, strengthened by **vetus**. *vetus* and *anticus* are not synonymous: *vetus* suggests that the practice has been around for a long time, whereas *anticus* tells us that it began a long time ago, as at 15.33. Postumus, to whom this poem is addressed, is unknown.

A S

21-2   alienum ... lectum is a 'bed belonging to another man' and the emphasis is placed on the powerful verb **concutere** ('to shake vigorously') which is emphasized in enjambement as an unsubtle euphemism for vigorous sexual activity: cf. Catullus 6. 11–12. After the crude imagery of this verb the tone becomes mock-religious as he mentions 'showing disrespect to the divine spirit of the sacred couch'. The *fulcrum* was literally the bed-head but is here synecdochic for the bed itself, while the term *genius* (the protecting spirit of a household) alludes to the procreative power of the Roman family and the threat to it constituted by adultery.

23-4   The section ends with the didactic point that adultery emerged before other vices. The sequence of 'ages' of mankind was first expounded by the early Greek poet Hesiod (*Works and Days* 109–201) and comprised four eras of diminishing moral integrity: gold, silver (**argentea**), bronze and finally iron (**ferrea**). **saecula** here is 'poetic' plural as there was only one silver age. **mox** means 'in due course': the time gap between the silver and the iron age was considerable. The passage and the sentence end with the strong noun **moechos**: a transliterated Greek word meaning properly 'a man who commits adultery' which thus shifts the blame for sexual misbehaviour momentarily from women to men. It will soon revert back to the women.

25–37

Are you intending to get married, Postumus? Are you insane? Better to commit suicide or to have sex with a boy.

25   Three formal elements of the marriage are listed here in an indignant catalogue of nouns which (the poet argues) are entrapping the foolish Postumus: the **conventum** ('meeting') is when the two families get together to agree the union, the **pactum** is the agreement entered into by both sides, while **sponsalia** refers to the betrothal ceremony itself. **nostrā** is to be taken with **tempestate** (here a more poetic word than *tempore* for 'time') in the next line.

26–7 The poet now provides vivid imagery of the wedding itself. The bridegroom has a haircut at the hands of a 'master' (**magistro**) barber for his special day, and the speaker shows his indignation with spitting alliteration of 'p' and 'd' in **pecteris ... digito pignus ... dedisti**. The 'pledge' (**pignus**) was an engagement ring (*anulus pronubus*), sent by the bridegroom to his fiancée as a sign of his fidelity. The word **fortasse** ('perhaps') here shows incredulity that Postumus has let things go so far, and also reminds us that the speaker does not know how far things have gone: if (after all) Postumus has already married, then his advice will be too late.

28–9 The poet's outrage is well conveyed in a tricolon crescendo: two short sentences making up line 28 and then the third limb taking up the whole of 29. The first is a statement, the second a rhetorical question and the third a direct command (**dic** – the singular imperative of *dico*) with effective anaphora and polyptoton of **qua ... quibus**. **exagitere** is the second person singular present passive subjunctive of *exagito* – subjunctive as it is an indirect question after **dic**. **sanus** ('healthy' or 'sane') has the specific sense of 'free from romantic infatuation' which is apt here. *uxorem <in matrimonium> ducere* is the formal phrase for a man marrying a wife.

29 Tisiphone, Megaera and Allecto were the three Furies or Erinyes – female divine spirits of vengeance who inflicted madness to punish human wrongdoing (as at Virgil *Aeneid* 7.415–60) and who are often shown with snakes (**colubris**) in their hair. For more details see *OCD* s.v. 'Erinyes'. Tisiphone is here used as a synonym for 'madness' as is clear from the ablative of instrument (**qua**) rather than an ablative of agent (*a qua*).

AS

30-3 Suicide (couched in a rhetorical question with reassuring language) is proposed as preferable to marriage: there are plenty of available (**salvis**) ropes, windows are wide open (**pateant**) and you do not have to go far to find the bridge which is 'neighbouring' (**vicinum**) and which positively offers itself for the purpose (**se praebeat**).

30   restibus ('ropes') refers to hanging which was a cheap and easy way to commit suicide. **dominam** is a key word – for a Roman man to be effectively enslaved by a woman (as Hercules was to Omphale in mythology) was an intolerable slight to his masculinity – and it is revealing to see how the speaker assumes that any wife will by definition be a **dominam**. **ullam** is poised at the end of the line for added effect and suggests that the speaker cannot stand 'any' mistress, however good.

31-2 Throwing oneself down from a great height was another way to end one's life, here referred to simply by mentioning the high places available.

31 The language is vivid: the windows have to be high (**altae**) to cause death, and **caligantes** adds extra force by alluding to the dizzying effect of vertigo, here transferred from the human self-defenestrator to the windows themselves.

32 The Aemilian bridge (the first stone bridge over the river Tiber, built in 179 BCE) was a good place from which to drown oneself: this method of suicide was (however) less favoured because it might well prevent the body being found and thus buried. The final monosyllable **pons** throws the rhythm off course and suggests the sudden plunge into the water.

33   exitus literally means a 'way out' and is euphemistic for death by suicide: **multis** alludes to the many alternative methods of self-despatch.

A S

34–5 Sleeping with a boy is better (**melius**) than being married to a woman – a disingenuous argument which proves that this speaker is an unreliable authority as well as a misogynist. The word **pusio** – a colloquial term from the same root as *puer* – refers to a young male catamite and is here repeated in epanalepsis from the fifth foot of line 34 to the first foot of 35.

35–7 The list of things which the boy does *not* do is a foretaste of the things which wives will be shown doing later on in the poem.

35 litigat is a legal term meaning 'to go to court' but here is used metaphorically for the verbal wrangling with which wives waste time and energy at night (see 268–9 below). The juxtaposition of **litigat exigit** neatly denotes the incessant nagging.

36 *munusculum* (the diminutive form of *munus* ('gift')) evokes the wheedling tone of the wife. **iacens** is a good word here: it suggests that the wife/boy is passively lying there, and looks forward to the next line in which the man is depicted as doing all the exhausting work. The rhythm of **nec queritur quod**, with its clash of ictus and accent as at 32, also suggests the panting which is to be spelled out in **anheles**.

37 The *latus* (the 'flank' or 'side' of the body) is commonly used of the bodily parts exhausted by sex: see 6.O19, Catullus 6.13. **parcas** and **anheles** are both subjunctives as they are reporting what the boy is (not) saying. The verb **iussit** picks up the theme of intolerable submission from **dominam** in 30.

38–81

And yet Ursidius, the seasoned adulterer, has decided to marry and have children and is looking for a good old-fashioned wife from the countryside. He will not find a good wife – certainly not in Rome where the women are all obsessed with dancers and actors. If his wife bears him a child it will be born looking like the gladiator who produced it.

AS

38   The *lex Julia de maritandis ordinibus* of 18 BCE and the *lex Papia Poppaea* of CE 9 were enacted to encourage marriage and the rearing of legitimate children (see Treggiari, *Roman Marriage*, 60–80). The identity of Ursidius is unknown.

38–9   **tollere** (literally 'to pick up') may refer to the tradition whereby a Roman father would pick up an infant and thus acknowledge his paternity, but is also a standard word for 'bringing up' children. *dulcis* is a word often used of beloved offspring (Horace *Epodes* 2.40, Lucretius 3.895, 4.1234) but here has a sarcastic edge as the satirist goes on to spell out the superior advantages offered by legacy-hunters. Many Romans wished to have a legitimate (male) heir to inherit the family estate (see e.g. Catullus 68. 119–24) and sterility in women was grounds for divorce (Treggiari, *Roman Marriage*, 462).

39–40   **cariturus** (the future participle of *careo*) has concessive force here: 'even though it will mean he has to go without . . '. The turtle dove was a renowned delicacy – and the adjective **magno** shows that this was a plump specimen – and the bearded mullet was a prized fish for the dinner-table. Note here the epic-style periphrasis whereby the poet refers to 'the beards of mullets' when he means 'bearded mullets' – followed by the personification which credits the market-place itself (**macello**) with being the legacy-hunter (**captatore**) when it is really human *captatores* who haunt the market in search of choice goods to use as bribes.

41–2   Postumus is addressed with another rhetorical question, using the figure known as the *adynaton* ('impossible') in which the achievement of one seemingly impossible feat makes all other things possible, however unlikely – if this man can marry, then anything can happen. **iungitur** (literally: 'is joined') has the specific sense of 'joined in marriage': Ursidius was not averse to female company in itself, as **moechorum** (see 23–4n.) makes clear. The surprise is given extra weight by the enjambement of **Ursidio**.

42-3 Key oppositional terms bring out the contrast between Ursidius' past and present status. The one-time (**olim**) adulterer now (**iam**) tamely submits to the halter of marriage (**maritali**). The *capistrum* was a harness put around the head of an animal in training: here the man is actively submitting (**porrigit**) to this treatment rather than being the passive beast being trained. **stulta** (stressed at the start of the line, and to be taken with **ora**) makes the poet's feelings plain and also looks forward to the following line, as *stultus* was the term for the stock figure of the cuckolded husband in the Roman 'adultery' mime (see next note).

44 Latinus was an actor at the court of the emperor Domitian, famous for playing the part of the lover who has to hide in a chest (**cista**) to escape the wrath of the husband who has returned unexpectedly and surprised his wife and her lover meeting in secret. **perituri** does not necessarily imply that a cuckolded husband might kill his wife's lover: here it simply means 'to be in for it' as often in comedy (*OLD* s.v. 'pereo' 5) – and the word also means to 'vanish from sight' which makes excellent sense of the juxtaposition with **texit** and **cista**. The adultery mime was sufficiently well-known for Juvenal to be able to evoke it here without further explanation.

45 **quid quod et . . .?** is a rhetorical expression ('what of the fact that also . . .?') to introduce a further consideration: the tone is one of hectoring banter as the speaker finds further ammunition for his condemnation of Ursidius' behaviour, whose folly in seeking a wife is worsened by his demand (at odds with his previous debauched behaviour) that the wife is to be of 'old-fashioned character'. **de** + ablative means simply 'made of' as at 5.165 (*OLD* s.v. 'de' 8). 'Old-fashioned' (**antiquis**) in Juvenal implies 'morally virtuous': the poet (like many ancient Romans) assumes that the past was an age of better, stronger people living more virtuous lives. **illi** is a dative of agent going with **quaeritur** in 46.

AS

46 **quaeritur** is stressed as the last word of the question and first word of the line: simply to *look* for such a wife is evidence of insanity. *pertundere venam* means to 'perforate a vein' and **nimiam** (going with **venam**) means 'oversized' and hence 'swollen (with excess of blood)'.

47 **delicias** (an accusative of exclamation) is used of over-the-top affectation at 260 below. The **Tarpeium limen** refers to the threshold of the Capitoline temple of Jupiter, Juno and Minerva, but also recalls the notoriously wicked woman Tarpeia who betrayed the Capitol to the enemy Sabines and was crushed to death under their shields as punishment (see *OCD* s.v. 'Tarpeia'). The speaker rounds on Postumus with two peremptory imperatives (**adora . . . caede**): **pronus** alludes to the fact that worshippers lay face down and kissed the threshold of the temple when engaged in worship (**adora**).

48 It made sense to worship Juno (the goddess of marriage) in gratitude for the virtuous wife he is hoping for: the worship here takes the form of the slaughter of a heifer (**iuvencam**) which has had its horns gilded (as at Virgil *Aeneid* 9.627).

49–50 *contingo* + dative in 49 has the sense of 'falling to one's lot' or 'being granted by fortune' (*OLD* s.v. 'contingo' 8): in line 50 it has its more literal meaning of 'to touch'. *caput* (literally 'head') commonly means 'person' as here: the emphasis is thrown onto the two following words **matrona** (a (potential) married woman) and 'chaste' (**pudici**).

50 **adeo** has the sense 'so true is it (i.e. that chaste wives are rare)'. The harvest goddess Ceres was especially associated with chastity: the procession at her festival in August involved women wearing white woollen bands or 'chaplets' (**vittas**), and so the speaker is asserting that few women are worthy even to touch these objects – let alone take part in the festival. Supply *sunt* with this line.

51 The reason for their unworthiness is now spelled out in obscene innuendo. *osculum* – in contrast to the sexualized *basium* – denotes a chaste kiss, such as is exchanged between relatives, but in the case of a daughter whose mouth is polluted by oral sex becomes something to be feared. **timeat** is a generic subjunctive: these are the type of women to make their fathers fear their kisses.

51–2 The detailed preparations for the wedding are listed: tying a garland (**coronam**) to their doorposts and stretching out clusters of ivy-berries (**corymbos**) around the threshold.

53–4 The bride-to-be (*Hiberina*: 'Spanish woman') is rudely mocked here and described as one who would sooner be content with one eye than one man. In Roman tradition, being *univira* (married to only one man in her lifetime) was a term of great praise for a wife. **ocius** (literally 'more quickly') means 'more readily', and **extorquebis** has the sense of 'extract by torture' as at 6.624, 14.251 as well as hinting at 'gouging out' when we meet the phrase **oculo . . . uno**.

55 The addressee is imagined as objecting that a good woman *can* be found, in the shape of one living a chaste life on her father's estate. Here **fama** has its sense of 'repute' (cf. 500, *OLD* s.v. 'fama' 6a) and the indefinite **cuiusdam** (from *quidam*) suggests that the girl's identity is of less importance than her good name. **rure paterno** evokes the safe environment of 'father's estate' where paternal protection would preserve her honour, along with the notion that country folk are more morally upright than their urban peers.

56–7 These lines make good use of repetition for scornful effect. **viventis. vivat . . . vixit . . . vivat** is a neat rhetorical sequence of four different forms of *vivo*, while **agro** is reduced on repetition to the diminutive form **agello**. The sentence ends with **paterno**, picking up the same word from the end of 55.

56–7   Gabii and Fidenae are proverbially sleepy towns about twelve miles away from Rome: this girl will misbehave in any town, however quiet.

57   The most plausible explanation of **cedo** is that it means 'I yield to' or 'concede' (*OLD* s.v. 'cedo' 10) and that **agello paterno** is a quotation of the phrase used as part of the girl's *fama*: '<if she can live chastely there> then I grant you that 'father's smallholding' stuff'. This helps to explain the affectionate diminutive *agellus* ('little *ager*') as part of the sentimental language used of the virtuous small-holder. The following two lines will however raise unsavoury suspicions about the innocence of country-folk.

58–9   Rural locations such as mountains and caves saw their fair share of sexual activity in legend and myth, and Jupiter was renowned for his promiscuity with many lovers in many settings. The love-affair for which Mars is most famous is his adulterous relationship with Venus, while his seduction of a Vestal Virgin (Rhea Silvia) produced the twin founders of Rome, Romulus and Remus. The syncopated rhythm of the end of line 59 throws emphasis onto the monosyllabic **Mars** and perhaps suggests his thrusting virility. The point of **senuerunt** is to ask sarcastically whether the gods are now so old that they have lost their sexual potency.

60–2   Colonnades were covered walking areas, often with shops attached; **spectacula** covers a wide range of theatrical performances held in the several stone theatres in Rome.

60–1   **voto** here means 'wishes' or 'heart's desire'. **cuneis** ('wedges') refers to the wedge-shaped blocks of seats in the Roman theatre: **totis** has the sense of 'entire blocks of seats' being scanned by the man looking for potential wives.

62   The subjunctives **ames** and **possis** with **quod** show that this is a relative final clause – 'something to love ... and to be able to ...'. The neuter gender of **quod** may seem harsh when speaking of a girl, but is common in the macho language of hunting which Ovid had applied to the quest for a girl (e.g. *Ars Amatoria* 1.35, 45–50, 91–2). **securus** has the sense of 'free of anxiety about her fidelity'.

63 Bathyllus was said to have introduced the Romans to the 'pantomime' in 23 BCE – a show in which a solo dancer rendered mythological stories (Leda in this case, who was seduced by Jupiter in the form of a swan) to the accompaniment of vocal and instrumental music (see *OCD* s.v. 'pantomime'). The Bathyllus mentioned here is obviously a later performer who had taken his illustrious predecessor's name for professional purposes (or else Juvenal is using the name as a byword for 'a pantomime performer'). The term 'pantomime' is a transliteration of Greek ('imitating everything') and *chironomos* is another Greek word ('hand-moving') used here adverbially ('in pantomime fashion'): the speaker mocks the pretentious Greek terminology covering these indecent pleasures. The pejorative word **molli** means 'effeminate' or 'pliant': Bathyllus is a man playing a woman and his sinuous movements are certainly 'pliant'.

64   vesicae ('bladder') suggests incontinence on the part of Tuccia, but Juvenal elsewhere (1.39) uses the word for 'vagina' and so more directly sexual arousal may be indicated here. There is also a historical joke: Tuccia was a Vestal Virgin who proved her innocence on trial by carrying water in a sieve, and so this Tuccia is publicly failing the test by spilling her 'water'. **Apula** means 'girl from Apulia' and the designation is doubly relevant here: Apulia, in South-East Italy, was regarded as the home of good old-fashioned people where land is cheap (4.27) and people are hardy: but it was also known for its wolves (Horace *Odes* 1.33.7–8), which gives **gannit** (a word usually used of dogs) more force. Dogs were regarded as proverbially shameless in the ancient world not least because of their public displays of urination, defecation and sexual intercourse.

65   This line is probably not by Juvenal: it was not uncommon for early readers of a text to scribble notes in the margin which a later scribe misread as being words by the poet which needed to be added to the text: later scribes would then struggle to make these 'interpolations' fit the metre and the sense. Here the sense has to be something on the lines of: 'just as in an embrace, a sudden and pathetic long <howling>'.

66   **Thymele** was a leading actress under the emperor Domitian: her name (in Greek) means 'the stage'. This line is framed by the two strong verbs **attendit** (she pays attention) and **discit** (she learns from it) with repetition of her name across the caesura. **tunc rustica** is making the point that this highly sophisticated actress is clod-hoppingly inept when compared to Bathyllus: *rusticus* (literally 'from the countryside') is often (see note on 14.25–6) used to denote primitive and unsophisticated behaviour and attitudes, especially in sexual matters.

67–70   Women console themselves when the theatres are closed with mementoes of their favourite actors. Women of all classes were said to idolize (some) actors and even had sexual affairs with them.

67–8   **quotiens** means 'on every occasion when'. **aulaea** were stage curtains, lowered at the start of the performance to reveal the stage-scenery and raised at the end. **recondita cessant** is an effective juxtaposition to stress the notion of 'out of sight and out of action': **vacuo clausoque** in the next line similarly conveys the deserted and locked-up theatre.

68   The **fora** were the open places where courts were held: usually the courts had to compete with the noise and the music coming from the theatres.

69   The Plebeian Games were held from 4 to 17 November, while the **Megalesia** (in honour of the goddess Cybele) were held from 4 to 10 April. Other festivals took place between April and November, but the winter was closed season for the theatres and the women are accordingly **tristes**.

70 Accius was clearly a man who played the role of Dionysus/ Bacchus or one of his acolytes, as the *thyrsus* was a staff wreathed with ivy which was peculiar to Dionysus/Bacchus. The *persona* was the mask worn by actors to conceal their real identity and to allow them to play a variety of roles, while the **subligar** was a sort of 'jock-strap' worn by actors to conceal their private parts – especially necessary when they were playing female roles in pantomime and wearing diaphanous clothing. The list of items is of increasing sexual force: the *persona* represents the face, the *thyrsus* is a metaphorical penis – but the **subligar** has actually touched the real thing.

71–2 Urbicus was evidently a comic actor and Atellan farces were a popular form of lowbrow comic entertainment which often produced burlesque versions of mythology: so here the actor is playing Autonoe, who was a sister of Agaue and aunt of King Pentheus. When this king rejected Dionysiac worship, the god drove these women to murder him by tearing him limb from limb: there is an aptness here in the female audience-member being similarly bewitched by the performance. The *exodium* was a short farcical item put on at the end of a play as comic relief. **Atellanae** (understanding *fabulae*) is a genitive of definition – 'an after-piece consisting of an Atellan (farce)'. The sentence as a whole is framed by the names **Urbicus ... Aelia pauper**, and **pauper** shows that female infatuation was not confined to the rich.

73 **magno** is ablative of price: 'for a great amount of money', while **his** is a dative of agent, showing that the women are taking the initiative here. The **fibula** was a pin or ring which was inserted into the foreskin to make sexual intercourse impossible: it was imposed especially on singers as it was believed that sexual activity was bad for the voice. Chrysogonus was a *citharoedus* (a man who sang and accompanied himself on the lyre (*cithara*)) and his apparent sexual inaccessibility raises his price.

74–5 Hispulla was the name given to a woman of gigantic proportions at 12.11, and the name also suggests 'hairy' (*hispidus* as at 2.11) which together amounts to a gross caricature of the infatuated woman. The name was also borne by the aunt of Pliny's wife and so may indicate a woman of the upper classes. The juxtaposition (over the line-end) of **tragoedo/gaudet** shows the paradox that Hispulla takes *joy* from the *tragic* actor.

75 Marcus Fabius Quintilianus was a famous teacher of rhetoric: he stands here as a byword for an older, boring man who would not attract the ladies. **ut** (+ subjunctive) is not uncommon after *expecto* to mean 'to expect that ...' (see 6.239, 14.25, *OLD* s.v. 'exspecto' 2b).

76 Echion is a Greek name and the evidence suggests that the man bearing it was probably a slave – the name may be ironic here as the name in Greek means 'snake-man' and its original bearer was one of the *spartoi* who fathered Pentheus (71–2n.). **accipis uxorem** is legal language for 'to marry a wife' but also suggests 'accepting' someone who will turn out to be unacceptable.

77 The names in this line are again important. **Glaphyrus** was a famous piper in the age of Augustus and this man may have taken the name of his illustrious predecessor (cf. Bathyllus at 63): the name in Greek means 'elegant' and also suggests 'smooth-skinned' or 'effeminate' as was Bathyllus (**molli** 63: although being effeminate in no way precluded heterosexual vigour). **Ambrosius** means 'immortal, divine' and is both a stage-name for the performer and perhaps a focalization of how the ladies see him. A **choraules** was a musician who played wind-instruments to accompany singers.

78–9 The wedding celebration is evoked by the vivid details of the **pulpita** and the decorated door-posts (as at 51–2). A *pulpitum* was a platform put up to allow people to watch the procession of the bride from her father's house to that of her new husband: these platforms are **longa** rather than wide as the streets are narrow (**angustos**) and the crowds were expected to be large. Line 78 is (almost) a 'golden line' where the central verb is framed by two adjectives and two nouns, agreeing with each other in a pattern a-b-V-A-B. The verb **figamus** is a jussive subjunctive ('let us set up') as is **ornentur** ('let (the doorposts) be decorated'). Laurel was a plant used to celebrate victory. Line 79 is marked by a sequence of heavy syllables, where only the fifth foot is dactylic: this suggests the slow pace of the forthcoming procession.

80–1 The wedding was ostentatious and the resulting child is also treated to lavish goods. *conopeum* (from the Greek word for a 'mosquito') seems to mean an infant's cradle complete with protective net. **testudineo** indicates that this cradle was inlaid with a tortoise-shell veneer – a mark of expensive luxury. Lentulus is a Roman name of some distinction: the Cornelii Lentuli were an old aristocratic family descended from the consul of 201 BCE. Line 80 is marked by the poetic use of apostrophe, where a character is addressed in the second person as if he were present (cf. 6.7), and also by the heavy fifth-foot spondee in **conopeo**.

81 This line is a devastating conclusion to this long sentence: after all that fuss over the wedding, the end-result is that a gladiator impregnates this man's wife and the cuckolding and the parentage are embarrassingly clear for all to see in a society where resemblance to the father was seen as proof of maternal fidelity. The line is framed by the **nobilis ... infans** – where **nobilis** is ironic considering his real parentage but would be apt for a legitimate child of a Lentulus. The *murmillo* was a gladiator who fought wearing heavy armour (of shield and short sword) and a helmet showing the image of a fish. This gladiator has the epic name *Euryalus* recalling either the handsome and brave youth in Virgil (*Aeneid* 5.295, 9.179–81) or else the man who engaged in a spirited if unsuccessful boxing match in the funeral games for Patroclus (Homer *Iliad* 23. 676–99). The elegant verb **exprimat** is also well-chosen, being used of artistic expression, and the final word **infans** means both 'infant' and also 'without speaking' (as the negative of *fans* (from *fari* (to speak)), which is perfect for this silent proof of the wife's infidelity.

82–113

Eppia, the wife of a senator, ran away with a gladiator called Sergius to Egypt, making light work of the hazards and discomfort of the sea-voyage. She would not have endured this if Sergius – who is not good-looking – were not a gladiator.

This section of the poem can be read as a burlesque version of myth and history, recalling the tales of Helen of Troy (who eloped with her lover Paris over the sea to Eastern lands (and in some versions ended up in Egypt)) and also Ariadne (who abandoned her Cretan family to sail off with Theseus). The poet is also aiming closer to home: it was expected of a Roman senator's wife that she would accompany him into exile if he were condemned, and this tale is a perversion of that tradition.

82　The line is sardonic: *comitor* is the usual verb for accompanying a husband or friend into exile, and **nupta senatori** ('married to a senator') leads us to expect that Eppia joined her husband in his suffering – only to find her going off with a troupe of gladiators (with **ludum** placed for effect at the end of the line).

83　Juvenal expresses contempt and distaste for Egypt, most notably in *Satire* 15. Pharos was an island close to Alexandria famous for its lighthouse, while the Nile was the river whose summer flooding was a wonder to the ancients and which guaranteed the double harvests which made the place so wealthy. Lagus was the father of Egypt's first Ptolemaic ruler in the fourth century BCE, and his name was applied to his capital Alexandria. The term *famosus* simply means 'an object of *fama* (public discussion)' and could mean 'legendary' or 'famed' when applied to the epic-sounding **moenia Lagi**, but the following line shows the pejorative sense of the *fama* of the place.

84 This line is an ablative absolute with **prodigia ... urbis** as the object of the verb **damnante**. A *prodigium* was an occurrence which inspired awe and wonder. Here the land full of wonders is itself shocked at the 'wonder' from Rome which is Eppia – a woman who scandalizes even the scandalous Egyptians. **prodigia et mores** is a hendiadys – where a single idea is expressed through two parallel nouns – meaning 'monstrous morals'. Canopus was a resort twelve miles from Alexandria, famous for its hedonistic lifestyle and debauched ways. The 'city' (**Urbis**) refers to Rome.

85–6 The moral condemnation of Eppia's neglect of family duty and insensitivity to shame is hammered home. The whole household (**domus**) could suffer from the scandal of her adultery: her husband (obviously) but also her sister (**sororis**) whose share-price as a potential wife herself would no doubt fall. The speaker adds vivid touches such as the 'weeping' (**plorantes**) children (**natos**) verbally surrounding this wicked woman (**improba**), and he even brings Rome herself into the list of sufferers, here called the 'fatherland' (**patriae**), the term suggestive of the patriarchal system which her actions were undermining.

87 The third line of this sentence undercuts the previous two with a sardonic and bathetic anticlimax. Leaving her family was surprising, but to leave her favourite pantomime actor and the Games was even more astonishing. This move from the sublime to the ridiculous is both entertaining and also moralistic in its judgement of Eppia's emotional shallowness. There may also be a light joke in that this modern Helen of Troy is leaving her 'Paris' for a man even less of a man than the original Trojan Paris. **utque magis stupeas** is a final clause addressed to the reader ('to make you even more amazed').

88–9 Eppia's luxurious upbringing makes her ability to withstand the discomfort of the voyage all the more amazing, and is a world away from the cave-woman's bed in lines 5–7. **pluma** means 'feather' and stands for the 'down' (from geese and swans) which was used in rich households to stuff mattresses. *cunae* ('cradle') is often used as a byword for one's infancy, while *segmenta* are pieces of expensive cloth stitched onto coverlets to enhance the luxury: the phrase as a whole evokes the rich and comfortable world in which Eppia lived as a little girl (**parvula**). The subjunctive after **quamquam** suggests that this is reflecting what people are saying about her.

90 The chiasmus here juxtaposes **pelagus** and **famam** as the objects of her disdain, and the rhetorical repetition of **contempsit . . . contempserat** reflects the fact that her scorn for her good name reflected and enabled her scorn for the sea. **olim** here means 'long ago' as at 14.180.

91 **cuius** picks up **famam**: the genitive is to be taken with **iactura**, so that phrase means 'the loss of which is of no importance'. **cathedras** (another Greek word) are 'chairs' and the adjective **molles** ('soft' or 'feminine') shows that these are cushioned ladies' seats, here used in synecdoche for the ladies themselves.

92–3 The 'Etruscan' (**Tyrrhenos**) waters are those off the western coast of Italy: she will have sailed south through the Straits of Messina into the 'Ionian' Sea to the east of Italy. **lateque sonantem** is an epic-sounding phrase for the 'far-resounding' sea which helps to emphasize Eppia's heroic bravery, along with the phrasing showing her endurance (**pertulit**) and her unflinching courage (**constanti pectore**).

93–4 **mutandum** is a gerundive of obligation agreeing with **mare**. Eppia's journey to Egypt was in fact a single voyage which involved traversing four stretches of water with four different names, with **totiens** emphasizing the number of such 'changes'.

94–7 Women who are travelling for honourable reasons (**iusta …
ratio … et honesta**) show fear, whereas women who are bold and
disgraceful (**turpiter audent**) do not. Women as a sex are generalized
as 'they' in the string of third-person plural verbs (**timent … gelantur
… possunt … praestant … audent**), and there is expressive
alliteration of 't' and 'p' for added rhetorical effect. The stereotype
assumes that noble women are suitably feeble.

94–5 **pericli … ratio** here means 'a reason <for incurring> danger'.
iusta and **honesta** are not synonyms: the former has the sense of
'morally right' while the latter indicates 'socially acceptable'.

95–6 The virtuous women's timorousness is described with a
tricolon of vivid language: first the simple verb (**timent**), then the
metaphor of 'freezing' (**gelantur**) in their hearts, and finally their
sheer incapability of even standing up on their 'shaking feet'. Line 96 is
neatly framed with **pectore … plantis**, conveying the totality of their
physical distress.

97 The climax is conveyed in a line of great power, framed by words
for 'daring' (**fortem animum … audent**) but dominated by the adverb
turpiter which colours their bravery as disgraceful.

98 The phrase is a mixed conditional, where the subjunctive protasis
(the 'if' phrase) is unreal but the indicative apodosis is presented as a
certainty. A husband might *not* tell his wife to sail, but (if he does so)
then her reaction is not in doubt.

98–9 The 'normal' female reaction to the idea of sailing is well
conveyed in a tricolon of ascending pain from simple embarkation
(**conscendere navem**) to the sickening (**gravis**) bilge-water (**sentina**),
to the attack of nausea as the sky 'wheels around'.

100 The adulteress goes after (**sequitur**) her lover of her own
volition – unlike the more virtuous wife who would need to be

ordered (**iubeat**) as in line 98 – and 'has a strong stomach' (**stomacho valet**) unlike her queasy counterpart.

100–2   The contrast between the two types of woman (**illa … haec**) is vivid. The one who is with her husband 'spews over him' (**convomit**, stressed in enjambement) while the eloping lover manages to eat (**prandet**), walk on board and even handle the ropes. The phrasing is well chosen throughout: **errat per puppem** shows her walking as she wishes throughout the ship and not simply where she must: she keeps company with the sailors (**inter nautas**) and is even happy (**gaudet**) to join them in their nautical tasks. There is also prurient sexual disapproval here: sailors were a byword for randiness and are lumped together with thieves, runaway slaves and executioners (8.174–5) as low-life – and the description of the adulteress being 'happy to take hold of their stiff (**duros**) cables (**rudentes**)' is clearly intended as an innuendo.

103   **qua … qua** is a strong anaphora: cf. 28–9n. The sentence reads: 'captivated (**capta**) by what (**qua**) beauty, what youth, did Eppia blaze with passion?' and is an indignant question, since Sergius was neither young nor beautiful (see 105–6n.).

104–5   **ludia** (from *ludus*) means 'a female slave attached to a gladiatorial school' who served the sexual needs of the men (see also 266): Eppia endured (**sustinuit**) being called (**dici**) by this opprobrious title, and the phrasing at 82–3 also suggested that she was going with a whole troupe (*ludum*) rather than one man.

105–6   **forma** and **iuventa** in line 103 are now debunked: far from being young, this man is in fact close to retirement age (**requiem**) and has begun to shave (**radere guttur**) which was only done once the white hairs had begun to sprout in the young man's beard (see 14.216–17), and **radere guttur** is a fittingly aggressive way to describe this swordsman's shaving habits. The gladiator has seen active service and his scars (**secto … lacerto**) are (he hopes) his ticket to retirement as they must have impaired his fighting ability – and yet Eppia calls him by the pet name **Sergiolus** (affectionate diminutive of *Sergius*) which neatly focalizes her fond idealization of him.

107–9 The facial disfigurements are many (**multa**) and three are listed in a rising tricolon of vivid hyperbole, with the key nouns (**sulcus ... gibbus ... ocelli**) at the beginnings and end of lines. The **sulcus** (literally 'furrow') is a deep scar from years of wearing a helmet and/or injury, while the **gibbus** – literally a hump on the back (cf. 10.294, 10.309) – is here a lump on his nose, its central position (**mediis**) and its size (**ingens**) making it impossible not to notice. The third flaw is the constant weeping of his eye, here (again) made absurdly mock-sentimental and affectionate by the use of the diminutive **ocelli** (for *oculi*: cf. line 8): the diminutive also marks a contrast with the **ingens** lump. Sergius probably suffered from *lippitudo*, a form of eye-infection common in ancient Rome (cf. e.g. Horace *Satires* 1.5.30) which could cause the eyes to stick closed and was certainly a nasty (**acre**) thing to suffer (**malum**) as well as an unattractive facial feature.

110 'But he was a gladiator <and so was attractive by virtue of that, despite his age and ugliness>'. **hoc** picks up the previous sentence ('this fact makes them (i.e. gladiators) into Hyacinthuses'). Hyacinthus was a beautiful youth from Sparta who was loved by the god Apollo and accidentally killed by the god with a discus – after which his eponymous flower sprang from his blood (see *OCD* s.v. 'Hyacinth'). The four-syllable Greek name here adds exotic colour to round off this study of Eppia's folly and delusion.

111–12 The language of 85–6 is repeated to mark the closure of this passage, with indignant plosive alliteration, anaphora of **hoc** at the start of the line and after the caesura, and the hapless cuckolded husband (**viro**) held over to the following line, showing him as an afterthought in the verse as well as in life. The speaker generalizes

AS

from this particular woman to the female sex as a whole (**amant**: 'they' love) and uses the single word **ferrum** to stand for the glamour of male violence displayed in the arena.

112–13   In a return to pragmatic reality, Eppia's lover Sergius is here given his real name instead of the sentimental diminutive (**Sergiolus** 105) by which she is accustomed to address him. He is now compared with **Veiiento** (in the same position on the next line), just as the sexy **ferrum** is replaced with the less sexy wooden sword (**rude**), which was given to gladiators as a mark of their retirement. **Veiiento** is presumably Eppia's husband: once retired, the glamorous hulk would be no more attractive than the senatorial husband she was leaving. **coepisset** is a neat touch: the transformation would not be instant or sudden.

114–241: Such scandals even happened in the emperor's own palace in the case of Messalina. Women will do anything to satisfy their lust and supposedly happy husbands must have their own ulterior motives (such as money or sex) for staying married – and good women are intolerably proud anyway. Some women are mad on all things Greek: and don't get married unless you want to be treated like a slave in your own home. Their mothers also connive at their infidelity.

242–5   *Women are the cause of legal wrangling.* The litigious woman is regarded here as a contradiction in terms, as the law was almost exclusively a male preserve. Women of this kind both pervert their own sex and also subvert masculine roles.

242   The poet overstates massively: **nulla ... in qua non** amounts to saying that all cases are started by women, even if men are the ones who do all the legal legwork. The juxtaposition of **femina litem** expresses outrage at women invading the male domain of the lawcourts.

243   **moverit** is a potential subjunctive (a woman 'could' start proceedings: cf. **sumpserit** at 266). There is an expressive juxtaposition of **moverit accusat**, enacting the instant process from starting the case to making the accusation. If she is not involved in making legal mischief, then (it is assumed) the woman is the target of a legal case as a **rea** (defendant) herself. Manilia is not known.

244–5 These women are experts in legal business and know enough to compose the legal briefs (**libellos**) for the advocate to make his case, and they are prepared to tell even a legal expert such as Celsus what to say and when to say it: **principium** refers to the opening speech, while **locos** are the separate 'points' to be made in the substance of the attack. Aulus Cornelius **Celsus** lived about a century before Juvenal and was an authority on legal rhetoric as well as a famous medical writer: for a man to advise him would be surprising, but for a woman to do so is monstrous. The surprising gender of the litigants is stressed by the phrase **ipsae per se** and by the concluding feminine participle **paratae**.

246–67 *Women even engage in gladiatorial training with a view even to fighting in the arena.* Gladiatorial combat was quintessentially masculine and for a woman to do this was (for this speaker) an abomination and a rejection of the female gender (253). Romans, in their constant quest for novelty in public entertainment, would vary the combat by having combinations of women, children and even dwarves acting as gladiators – but such performers were usually slaves or prostitutes. For upper-class women performing in the arena cf. Mevia who takes part in the beast-hunt 'with breast bared' at 1.22–3.

246 The line, framed by Greek nouns and with an unusual fifth-foot spondee, is a calculated sneer. The *endromis* was a simple track-suit worn by athletes while training: this female athlete insists on having hers dyed with expensive Tyrian purple, showing extravagance as well as a lack of femininity. **ceroma** refers here to the clay floor laid down for wrestling bouts, and the juxtaposition with **femineum** enhances

AS

the shock value of the phrase. The Greek terms suggest that this female behaviour is (yet) another instance of baleful Greek influence.

247   quis nescit indicates a rhetorical question, often used to mean 'we all know' – here amplified and elaborated with the parallel **quis non vidit**. The *palus* was a wooden post set in the ground and used by gladiators to practise sword-thrusts: **vulnera** ('wounds') humorously focalizes the activity as these would-be swordswomen inflict injuries – on a wooden pole.

248   The woman gouges holes (**cavat**) in the timber with a constant succession (**assiduis**) of blows from the wooden swords (**rudibus**) and assaults with the shield (here used as a weapon as well as a defensive barrier). The words for the weapons (**rudibus scutoque**) are juxtaposed in the middle of the line, framed by the strong indicative verbs. The subject of the verbs here is the **matrona** in 250.

249–50   numeros are the rhythmic training exercises used by athletes. The *Floralia* were games held annually from 28 April to 3rd May in honour of the goddess Flora. These games featured (sham) fighting bouts between prostitutes (who probably fought naked as befitted their status) to the sound of the trumpet (**tuba**). For a **matrona** (a respectable married woman) to train for this event was shocking.

250–1   si is pleonastic after **nisi** but *siquid* was treated as a single word meaning 'something' and the line would not have been so odd to a Roman reader. The **matrona** is (the speaker speculates) preparing herself for the 'real arena' (see note on 246–67) rather than the sham female fight at the Floralia. **paratur** is a 'middle' use of the passive, denoting 'preparing herself' rather than 'being prepared' (cf. *vertitur* (99)).

252   Mention of the helmet (an emblem of masculine valour) brings out the grotesque incongruity here, and the juxtaposition **galeata**

pudorem stresses and explains her disgrace. The plosive alliteration is suitably scornful.

252–3 **pudorem** denotes 'sense of shame' or 'modesty' and the need to avoid disgrace: cf. 6.357, 14.178. The joke here is this: shameless fighters run away from their enemy (cf. 2.144), but this one is running away from her own gender-role, with **sexu** placed last in the rhetorical question for emphatic surprise. There is a neat chiasmus also of **fugit a sexu? vires amat** where the contrasting verbs frame the contrasting nouns. At 112, the speaker generalized that all women love 'the blade' (**ferrum**): here this particular woman is (he surmises) in love with 'violence' (**vires**).

253–4 The speaker adds a dig at women's lust, alluding to the myth that women take 90 per cent of the pleasure of sex while men only feel the remaining 10 per cent: Ovid (*Metamorphoses* 3.316–38) narrates how the prophet Tiresias (who had been both male and female in his long life) was consulted by the gods on this contentious issue. The speaker sees this from the male viewpoint (**nostra**) with the exclamatory **quantula** ('how tiny!').

255 Understand *sit* with **quale decus. decus** (literally 'glory' or 'honour') is sarcastic here as a husband would be disgraced to have a wife with such gear: it is also ironic as weaponry is usually the outward sign of military glory. Selling off surplus family property was not uncommon in ancient Rome.

256–7 The items listed were used by the 'Samnite' form of gladiator: a sword-belt (**balteus**), arm-rings (**manicae**) to protect the sword-wielding right hand, the crest (**cristae**) on the helmet, and a metal greave (*ocrea*) worn on the left leg (**cruris ... sinistri**) which was the forward leg in the Samnite style of fighting. The top half of the leg was protected by the shield and so this is only a 'half' (**dimidium**) 'covering' (**tegimen**).

AS

257–8 'Thracian' gladiators wore greaves on both legs and so a wife fighting in that style would have twice as many greaves to sell. **vendente puella** is an ablative absolute, and we have to understand *eris* with **felix. felix** is ironic here (as at 10.248, 14.21), as no respectable husband would be 'happy' in this situation. **puella** suggests a young wife.

259–60 This woman is now accused of wearing immodest clothing: the *cyclas* was a light outer garment with a golden decorated border (described as **tenui** ('flimsy' or even 'diaphanous')) which suggested sexual availability. The *pannus* was a rag or shirt: the diminutive **panniculus** shows that this small garment is even smaller, and **bombycinus** ('silk' – from the word *bombyx* (silk-worm)) shows that it was made of the finest chiffon material which allowed the male gaze to see the female body underneath (cf. Martial 8.68.7). A woman who can fight in heavy armour nonetheless claims discomfort in the lightest feminine clothing, her **delicias** ('sensitive skin') being positively burned (**urit**: stressed at the end of the line and the sentence). The long words and the absence of a caesura in the third foot perhaps suggest her irritation with the garment.

261–4 The delicate creature is a virago in the arena. The reader is addressed with two imperatives (**aspice . . . ride**) and given a string of indirect questions pointing out the details (**quo . . . quanto . . . quanta . . . quam**). The speaker builds up the quasi-heroic description of the armour and its wearer, only to undercut it all with the bathetic comedy (**ride**) of the chamber-pot in 264.

261 The woman roars as she carries out the sword-thrusts (**ictus**) which have been demonstrated (**monstratos**) by her trainer.

262–3 A gladiatorial helmet weighed about 4kg, enough to make the woman 'bend' (**curvetur**) under it. The metal greaves would chafe the foot and the leg beneath it, and so gladiators protected their flesh with a bandage (**fascia**) made from tree-bark (*liber*). **denso ... libro** is an ablative of description going with **fascia**, and **quam** is to be taken with **denso**. **poplitibus** are 'knees' and would be the only part of the leg visible between the greave and the shield which protected the upper leg.

264 A **scaphium** was a woman's chamber-pot and the joke here is that the female fighter has to remove her armour (**positis ... armis**) to use it.

265–7 Gladiators do not let their own wives and girlfriends behave like the wives of noble Roman citizens. Here the speaker interestingly turns to addressing the women themselves (**neptes**) and arraigning them for their dissolute behaviour. The three family names mentioned are all bywords for the illustrious Roman past: the Aemilii Lepidi served Rome through many generations of consular rank, while L. Caecilius Metellus lost his sight (**caeci**) saving a statue from the burning temple of Vesta in 241 BCE. Q. Fabius Maximus Gurges (the 'glutton' – a name earned in his dissolute youth) was consul three times and a war-hero in the early third century BCE, and ironically exacted harsh punishment on married women found guilty of sexual misconduct (Livy 10.31.9). **-ve** added to the end of a word acts like **aut** before it: 'or blind Metellus'.

266–7 The section is concluded with two rhetorical questions, moving from the general ('what **ludia** ever ...?') to the particular (**uxor Asyli**), thus ending with the name of a gladiator, whose partner is ironically described as a proper **uxor** who would never 'grunt at the training-pole' (**ad palum gemat**): in real life of course gladiators were not allowed to marry and so the partner would be called a *contubernalis* rather than an *uxor*, but in the topsy-turvy world of satire these lowlifes treat their 'wives' better than citizens treat their legitimate spouses.

268–85

From fighting in the arena the speaker now turns to the constant fighting in the bedroom between husband and wife.

268   **lites** (literally 'lawsuits') here means 'quarrels' and were a wifely speciality (cf. 35), the hyperbole being enhanced by **semper. alterna ... iurgia** denotes 'mutual recriminations'.

269   A well-crafted line, framed by **in quo ... in illo** and with oxymoronic contrast of **iacet: minimum dormitur** separated by the caesura. **dormitur** is an impersonal passive.

270   The line makes a single point, first in plain terms and then with a vivid simile, the two phrases each introduced with anaphora of **tum ... tunc** and understanding *est*. The tigress has excellent reasons to be fierce as she is 'bereaved' (**orba**) of her cubs, but the wife is only feigning her feelings, as the next line shows.

271   The wife makes quarrelsome accusations to hide her own guilt, faking her grief while being all too aware (**conscia**) of her own 'secret doings'.

272   An adulterous wife invents lovers (either slave-boys (**pueros**) or a female mistress (**paelice**)) enjoyed by her (faithful) husband. **ficta paelice** is either ablative absolute ('having invented a mistress') or ablative of cause (she weeps 'over an invented mistress').

273–5   Tears are her key weapons, described over three lines: they are metaphorically personified as 'at the ready' (**in statione sua**), like soldiers who are ready and waiting (**paratis ... expectantibus**) for her orders (**iubeat**); and the adjective **uberibus** well conveys the gushing tear-ducts. Once again (cf. 268) the poet exaggerates with **semper**, here repeated for emphasis, and the hiatus in line 274 (where **suā atque** is not elided into **su'atque**) perhaps enacts the staccato sobs of the weeping wife (see Introduction page 3).

274–5   **illam** is the direct object of **expectantibus**, but the woman referred to is then the subject of **iubeat**, so that the phrase reads: 'waiting for her (**illam**) to tell them (**iubeat**) in what way (**quo . . . modo**) they are to flow'.

275–6   The indignation is shown in the anaphora, polyptoton and alliteration of **tu . . . tu tibi tunc**, in the sequence of gullibility from 'believing' that she loves him (**credis**) to being 'pleased' with himself (**places**) and 'kissing away her tears' (**fletum . . . exsorbes**), all conveyed in strong second person singular language in the present tense. The husband ironically takes pride in what he sees as her passionate love for him, not seeing that he is being fooled. **uruca** ('worm') is only found here as an abusive term but makes eminent sense as worms are as blind as this dolt.

276–7   There is effective word-placing and word-choice here. **exsorbes** is stressed in enjambement as the husband 'drinks up' the tears with his lips – although *exsorbeo* has an unsavoury tone, being used mainly for fluids such as blood and wine-dregs – and the affectionate diminutive **labellis** (in heavy contrast with the **tabellas** in the same position on the following line) neatly and ironically focalizes his sentimental feelings for her. **lecture** (the vocative masculine singular of the future participle of *lego*) is addressed to the husband who will read 'what' (**quae**) and 'how many' (**quot**) writing-tablets (**tabellas**) she has written.

278   **scrinia** are containers for book-rolls or for writing tablets which were used for love-letters. **zelotypae** is a direct transliteration of a Greek adjective meaning 'jealous' and also refers to a character in a Roman mime which shows that this lady is playing her theatrical role to perfection, while **moechae** ends the sentence and the line with the sordid truth (23–4n.). **tibi** is a dative of agent going with **retegantur**.

279–85 The speaker dramatizes the adulterous woman's behaviour from being caught in bed with a slave or knight, to seeking advice from an expert rhetorician, to hearing her plead her excuses to her husband.

279 Roman husbands were allowed to have sex with slaves but the same permission did not extend to their wives, although such liaisons obviously occurred (e.g. Tacitus *Annals* 12.53). Roman knights (*equites*) were men of substantial financial means who did not engage directly in politics.

279–80 The repetition of the imperative **dic**, along with the colloquial **sodes** ('please' formed from *si audes*) shows the impatient anxiety of the woman. **colorem** is a term for a positive 'spin' or argument to justify the unjustifiable. Quintilian (see 75n.) was an eminent professor of rhetoric.

281 Even Quintilian cannot think up a suitable excuse. **haeremus** (literally 'we are stuck') is a good term for 'we are lost for ideas' and **dic ipsa** (which redirects the demand for a defence back onto the woman) shows his irritation.

281–3 The wife pleads that there had been an agreement (**convenerat**, an impersonal use of the verb *convenio*) between them that they should both enjoy the same freedom to seek pleasure elsewhere, with **olim** suggesting that the agreement was of long standing. The wife describes the husband as allowed to 'do whatever you want', while she, with conspicuous understatement, was only asking 'to be able to indulge' herself – which is a monstrous euphemism for having sex with the slaves. **nec non** ('and furthermore' (cf. 14.130)) adds rhetorical dignity to her desperate pleading.

283 **licet** + subjunctive has concessive force: 'though you may …'. The phrase **mare caelo confundas** (literally: 'upset the sea with the sky') has the metaphorical sense here of 'though you bring the house down' (or some such).

284   The wife pleads that 'to err is human' – as well as suggesting that she deserves the same freedom as her husband.

284–5   Another generalization (cf. 94–7, 112) about women as being most 'daring' when they are caught out, explaining their anger (**iram**) and their confidence (**animos**) as being derived from their guilt: they are 'shameless' in both senses of the word. **deprensis** is placed for emphasis in enjambement and means '<if and > when they are caught <doing wrong>'.

286–305

The speaker now returns to the theme of the virtuous past and tells us that modern immorality is caused by the growth of luxury: comfort breeds boredom and mischief – see 14.160–88 for a similar treatment of this moralizing trope.

286   **unde** and **quo de fonte** are both asking the same question in different forms and we have to understand a verb such as *sint: fonte* is almost certainly a reminiscence of Horace ('from this source (*hoc fonte*) disaster was drawn' (*Odes* 3.6.19) and the language sets up an ironically pompous tone. **monstra** refers to the prodigious immorality shown by the women Juvenal has been describing (cf. **prodigia** at 84).

287–91   Women in the past (**quondam**) had no time or energy for sexual affairs as they were too busy dealing with work, lack of sleep and the threat of invasion. The argument is exaggerated – single events such as the invasion of Hannibal did not happen often, and having calloused hands never stopped anyone from having sex – but not without comic force.

287   **castas humilis** is a good juxtaposition of key words, but the assertion that women in the past were **castas** is at odds with his

AS

remark earlier (24) that adultery began in the 'silver' age. **Latinas** means 'Latin women'.

288–91   The word order allows the poet to state the fact of moral purity first (**nec ... tecta**) and then to list the contributing factors which explain it: (a) **labor** (b) **somnique breves** (c) **vexatae ... manus** (d) **Hannibal ... mariti.**

288   **contingi** ('to be touched') has the sense of 'stain' or 'pollute' (see 49–50n.). **parva** denotes the 'little' houses of these ancestral poor folk – a sentimental idealization of ancient poverty like *glebula ... casae* at 14.166–7. **sinebant** is important here: the moral values were not freely chosen but imposed on them by circumstances – as with the ugly cavewoman of 5–10, these early women were condemned to 'goodness' by a lack of opportunity.

289–90   Sleep was a luxury they could ill afford, and their hands were hardened (**durae**) and chafed (**vexatae**) by handling fleeces from Etruria (an area north of Rome). Wool-working was always a mark of the virtuous wife.

291   **Hannibal** the Carthaginian commander led his forces against Rome and in 211 BCE he approached close to (**proximus**) the city: Roman forces took up position in front of the walls between the Esquiline and the Colline gates and only heavy rain prevented a major battle that night (7.163–4, Livy 26.10). The point here is the final word **mariti** – their husbands were all engaged in defending the city and so wives perforce slept alone.

292–3   The surprising sentence makes an argument which was conventional in Roman times: peace is a good thing, but extended peace brings 'evils' (**mala**) which we are 'suffering' (**patimur**). The moralist might argue that fear of an enemy keeps people sober and attentive to honour, while the relaxed life of peace encourages people to indulge themselves in **luxuria**; the economist might point out that peace frees up money and the opportunity to engage in trade which brings in luxury goods and also encourages a softer lifestyle. The point is powerfully made by suggesting that the **luxuria** was 'more ferocious than weapons' and 'avenges the conquered world' by delivering moral 'wounds' which hurt and subdued Rome. The verb **incubuit** suggests the attack of a disease.

294–5　The 'death of poverty' is something we aspire towards, but which some Roman moralists regarded as a bad thing, bringing with it the twin evils of crime (**crimen**) and lust (**libidinis**). The verb **perit** is scanned *perīt*, the lengthened final syllable showing that this is a perfect tense (shortened from *periit*) and not present (which would be *perĭt*). **ex quo** understands *tempore*: 'from the time when'.

295–7　**hinc . . . hinc** is explanatory ('from this loss of poverty'). **fluxit ad istos . . . colles** is paradoxical: the metaphor of **fluxit** is one of 'flowing' and water flows downhill, but this stream of luxury has flowed 'to the hills (of Rome)'. The foreign influences which have polluted Roman poverty are here represented by significant places: **Sybaris** was a Greek colony in South Italy, destroyed in 510 BCE and a byword for extravagant luxury and sexy poetry (Ovid *Tristia* 2.417); the men in the Greek island of **Rhodes** were wealthy and 'unwarlike' (8.113); **Miletus** (in what is now Turkey) was a Greek city whose empire was said to have collapsed owing to their love of pleasure, while **Tarentum** (a Greek colony in South Italy) was called 'soft' and 'unwarlike' by Horace (*Satires* 2.4.34, *Epistles* 1.7.45). The incident recalled in line 297 occurred in 281 BCE: a Roman ambassador visited the city during a festival of Dionysus when the people were drunk (**madidum**) and garlanded (**coronatum**). One of their number dirtied the ambassador's clothing with excrement, an act well worthy of the adjective **petulans**.

298–9　'Filthy money' (**obscena pecunia**) is blamed for importing 'foreign ways' (**peregrinos . . . mores**) with some indignant plosive alliteration. Trade conducted with other nations for profit (along with empire-building and the removal of the military threat from Carthage) allowed the Romans to import goods and destructive 'foreign' ways.

299–300   The judgement becomes more pointed: this 'effeminate wealth shattered our times with disgusting luxury'. The plural **saecula** suggests the snowballing decline of generation after generation (as previously stated by Horace *Odes* 3.6.46–8) and **fregerunt** has the sense of 'broke the strength of' or even 'emasculated', with **molles** strongly suggestive of effeminacy and **turpi** a common word for deviant behaviour as at 97.

300–5   This section ends with a wonderful sketch of the drunken woman in the context of a banquet, embodying the moral and physical abandon which the previous lines have described. The emphasis here is on lack of control (**nescit**, the impersonal verb **bibitur**, the spontaneous movement of ceiling and table); and the passage focalizes the world through her drunken eyes.

300   **Venus** was the Roman goddess of sexual love and her name is used here by metonymy for sexual desire, as personified in an unnamed woman who is made promiscuous by drink.

301   The drunken woman has lost her judgement and uses her head (**capitis**) as much as her groin (**inguinis**) for sex.

302   The food is excessive and luxurious ('massive oysters'), the timing is decadent (**mediis iam noctibus**) and the eating is animalistic: **mordet** ('gnaws at') is not ladylike and is used at 15.87 of cannibals. Oysters were a prized delicacy in Roman times much enjoyed by the wealthy and Roman dinners (which started in the middle of the afternoon) would usually be over well before midnight.

303   The drink is similarly over the top: fine Falernian wine unmixed with water (**mero**) is itself mixed into perfumes (**unguenta**) and drunk from a perfume-shell (**concha**). Adding a small amount of perfume to a wine was not unknown, but here the excess is brought out by reversing the process so that the wine is added to the perfume rather than vice versa – like having tea with your sugar rather than sugar with your tea. The expressive verb **spumant** is central to the line and the juxtaposition of **unguenta Falerno** enacts the mixing process.

304–5 The impersonal passive **bibitur** ('drinking is taking place') neatly shows the erosion of her judgement: and the drinking produces dizziness and double-vision. The ceiling 'walks' (**ambulat**) with a 'dizzying motion' (**vertigine** – which is of course inside the woman's head), while the table 'gets up' (**exsurgit**) with 'double the number of lamps'.

306–51: The speaker describes the rites of the Bona Dea, where women go mad in an orgy of drunken lust. Women of all classes are equally debauched.

352–65 *Women are spendthrifts.* Ogulnia, an impoverished aristocrat, cannot afford to buy the gear which ladies usually take to the games and so wastes her scanty resources by hiring them (**conducit**, the verb emphasized by epanalepsis in 353). The speaker has already (60–72) described women's sexualized addiction to shows and performers: here he is looking at similar things from a worried husband's financial perspective.

352–4 The list of accoutrements is alarmingly long, its length emphasized by asyndeton in 353. Appearance matters most, hence dress (**vestem**) comes first: followed by the attendants (**comites**), the sedan-chair (**sellam**), the cushion (**cervical**: probably for use on the stone seating of the Roman theatre) and hired friends (**amicas**) along with a nanny figure (**nutricem**) and a slave-girl. This **puella** is possibly German, as shown by **flavam** (blonde: cf. 13.164–5 where blue eyes and blonde hair are seen as the norm in Germany), and she is there perhaps to deliver messages to the objects of Ogulnia's desire. The point of the expense is to look decent, but the indecent reason for her attending the games is made clear in the following lines.

355–6 She gives out whatever is left of the family silver (**argenti**) to 'smooth-skinned athletes'. Note here the reminder that this is a rich family fallen on hard times in **argenti . . . paterni** and then **vasa novissima** (the last remaining vases) all suggestive of old aristocratic property.

356 **lēvibus athletis** were young men who were not yet fully bearded; they used to perform athletics in the Greek style in Rome.

357 There is a neat generalizing contrast here of **multis . . . sed nulla**: 'many' women are poor but 'none of them' acts poor. **res angusta** here means 'shortage of property', while **multis** is a possessive dative understanding *est*. **pudorem** means 'shame, embarrassment' (in this case at their poverty: cf. 252–3n.) – which (the speaker claims) women lack altogether.

358–9 Prudent people restrict their expenditure to their income: this woman does not 'measure herself' (**se metitur**) to that limit (**modum**) which this (**haec**: i.e. poverty) has 'given and set down' (**dedit . . . posuitque**).

359–60 The speaker asserts that – unlike women – men 'occasionally' (**aliquando**) look out for (**prospiciunt**) what is useful (**utile quid sit**) in the future, and 'some of them' (**quidam**) fear poverty.

360–1 The harsh alliteration of 'f' here well evokes the fearful prospect of cold and hunger. The ant was a byword for frugal providence; in Aesop's fable the ant works hard all summer to lay up stores for the winter, and the idle grasshopper (who spends the summer singing) comes begging the ant for food when winter strikes. Men – unlike women – do eventually (**tandem**) come to their senses, claims the speaker: the verb **expāvēre** (from *expavesco*) is a so-called 'gnomic' perfect tense making a generalized statement, and the line is pompously spondaic. **formica ... magistra** is an ablative absolute.

362 A fine summary in a single line, framed with the key terms **prodiga** and **censum** ('estate', 'family wealth'), this last being personified as 'perishing' (**pereuntem**).

363 Money famously does not grow on trees, but this women acts as if the cash (**nummus**) is a living thing which is 'falling into the soil' (**recidivus**) and 'sprouting new growth' (**pullulet**) once the money-chest has been drained (**exhausta ... arca**: another ablative absolute).

364 The imagery of a 'pile' (**acervo**) of money (*OLD* s.v. 'acervus' 1b) is found often in Horace (e.g. *Satires* 1.1.44–51). The unreality of the situation is brought out by **semper**.

365 **quanti** is a genitive of price: 'how much' their pleasures cost.

366–97: Women bring into the house a motley crowd of people: perverts, eunuchs and musicians.

398–412

The poet discusses the busybody gossip, whose prurient curiosity extends to high matters of foreign policy and to the lowest details of other people's sex lives.

398 **cantet** and **pervolet** are both jussive subjunctives: 'let her be musical rather than fly around'. **Urbem** is the city of Rome.

399 **possit** is a generic subjunctive: 'the sort of woman who could ...'. For a woman to attend gatherings of males unrelated to her showed her to be outrageously bold (**audax**).

400–1 The *paludamentum* was a red, purple and gold cloak worn by a general when going off on campaign: for this woman to harangue such important men at such an inopportune moment was a sign of *audacia*. The presence of her husband (**praesente marito**) makes things worse as he should have been the one speaking, rather than the lady herself (**ipsa**). The ablatives in **recta facie siccisque mamillis** are ablatives of description: **recta facie** indicates that her gaze is brazenly forward and not cast down like that of a modest woman, while the 'dry breasts' perhaps indicates a lack of femininity.

402–3   The woman knows more than one would expect about what is going on all over the world (**toto fiat in orbe**), and in particular she is well up on foreign affairs relevant to the Roman empire. The Chinese (**Seres**) represent the far East, the Thracians the far North.

403–4   From the international to the interpersonal: the woman knows the secret (sexual) acts of a stepmother (**novercae**) and her stepson, her disapproval being shown in the noun **pueri**. The relationship amounted to incest and was explored in (e.g.) Euripides' *Hippolytus* and the tale of Bellerophon, who resisted the advances of his stepmother and was made to suffer by her (Homer *Iliad* 6.156–70). In those cases, the stepsons were virtuous and the woman wicked, but the guilt or innocence of the parties is here left open. **quis amet** simply means 'who is in love': while the final phrase of 404 depicts the adulterous man being fought over (**diripiatur**) by lustful females, recalling the figure of the *moechus* at 23–4, 42–4. **quis ... adulter** means 'which adulterer', with **quis** being used for the adjectival *qui*.

405–6   To impregnate a widow (**viduam**) was a sexual crime: this woman is prurient enough to calculate the month of conception (**quo mense**). **quaeque** (from *quisque*) means 'each and every' and so asserts (with the string of indirect questions (**quis ... quo ... quibus ... quot**)) that the gossip has an encyclopaedic knowledge of every woman's sexual behaviour, both verbal and physical. **modis** indicates sexual positions.

407-12 The busybody acts as a walking newspaper, relaying world events in ever more garish language.

407 Comets were often seen as accompanying major events such as the births and deaths of great men and also regime changes: hence this comet is 'threatening' the kings of Armenia and Parthia. Trajan, who was campaigning in Armenia in 114 to remove the upstart Parthamasiris from the throne and turn Armenia into a Roman province, went on to fight in Parthia in 116, ousting the king and replacing him with a Roman appointee before Trajan's own death in 117. A comet was witnessed in November 115 – too late for the Armenian campaign but possibly 'threatening' trouble for the Parthian king. This woman is of course more concerned with a good story than with chronological exactness.

408 **prima videt** is stressed in enjambement and lends a touch of absurdity to her claims – while **prima … recentes** neatly frame the line with emphasis on the 'latest news'.

409 She 'picks up' (**excipit**) some stories at the gates of the city and just invents others (**quosdam facit**). The following words are a series of accusatives and infinitives in breathless indirect statement, showing her relish of each gory detail. The Niphates is a mountain range in Armenia but this woman (like some Roman writers) thinks it is a river: it is apt that this woman is not so well-informed as she thinks.

410-11 The disasters unfold in graphic detail with the (fictitious) movement of Niphates stated simply (**isse**) and then followed by hyperbolic details of its attacking whole peoples (**in populos**), as 'all the fields' (**cuncta arva**) are gripped by a 'massive flood' – with the enjambed key word **diluvio** overspilling the line as the water overspills the land.

411 There was an earthquake in Antioch (in Syria) in December 115 which is presumably what the woman is describing here as the cities 'totter' (**nutare**) and the lands 'sink' (**subsidere**).

A S

412   The woman is indiscriminate in her storytelling as is stressed by the 'whichever … whoever' words **quocumque … cuicumque**. The passage ends with the key word **narrat**, often used of telling tall stories (cf. 15.14).

The rest of the poem describes other sorts of women: the angry wife, the argumentative wife, the wives who love jewellery too much or are cruel to their slaves, the superstitious wives who employ fake fortune-tellers, the ones who procure abortions or import into the house other people's babies as their own, and wives who harm their husbands with love-potions. The poem ends with murderous wives who murder their children and their husbands.

Satire 14

This long poem begins with a satirical look at bad parenting in general (1–106) before moving on to the specific case of avarice and its disastrous effects on family and society (107–331).

1–58

Parents should set a good example to their children if they wish them to grow up into good citizens.

1–3 plurima, qualified by the two phrases **et fama . . . sinistra** and **et nitidis . . . rebus**, leads to the relative clause **quae monstrant . . . parentes**.

1 plurima is an adjective acting as a noun ('very many things'). **Fuscinus** is otherwise unknown and is probably a significant name (*fuscus* means 'dark' and so this man is 'shady'). **fama digna** could be positive ('worthy of renown') but this is overturned with the pejorative **sinistra** – the children will suffer 'harmful gossip'.

1–2 et . . . et . . .: two parallel defining phrases effectively say the same thing ('damaging their reputation') in different terms.

2 haesuram (future participle of *haereo*) goes with **maculam**. Notice the metrical effect as the dactyls of the first part of the line are suddenly slowed down as the stain 'sticks', and also the oxymoronic juxtaposition of **nitidis maculam**, where **nitidis** ('shining bright' as at 6.8) is a foil for the black mark (**maculam**).

3 Young people are commonly said to be led astray by Roman society, by bad company or bad teachers – but here it is the parents themselves (**ipsi**) who are corrupting their own children. **monstrant** suggests demonstration (cf. 10 below) of habits and could be done by anybody, while **tradunt** often means 'leaving as a legacy' and so fits well with **parentes**.

A Level

4–5 The vivid and picturesque details of gambling look forward to the avarice and extravagance which is the focus of much of the rest of the poem (107–331). **alea** was gambling with dice, while the *fritillus* was the box for shaking (and then throwing) the dice; the word **damnosa** here indicates recklessly high stakes. The child has a suitably pint-sized (**parvoque**) dice-box and the speed of the imitation of his elders is enacted in the close succession of **iuvat alea ludit**.

5 The *bulla* was a locket or charm worn by boys until they came of age: the passive participle **bullatus** means 'wearing the *bulla*' (cf. *paludatis* at 6.400). The line is framed by the vivid terms **bullatus** and **fritillo**, the latter word sounding suitably diminutive (although it is not in fact a diminutive form) and having an onomatopoeic ring for the rattling dice-box. The serious competition and the lethal losses involved are evoked in the military metaphor of **movet arma**.

6–7 The **iuvenis** will not allow (**concedet**) any of his relatives to entertain hopes (**sperare**) about him (**de se**).

7 The speaker moves from extravagance in gambling to extravagance in food. **tubera terrae** are truffles, a delicacy enjoyed as a dessert after a main meal of goose, capon and boar at 5.116. The youth has learned to peel (**radere**) them himself in case a clumsy chef removes too much of the precious fungus.

8–9 The *boletus* was a delicious mushroom and the fatally favourite dish of the emperor Claudius (6.620–3, Suetonius *Claudius* 44.2, Tacitus *Annals* 12.67). **condire** (to 'marinade') was evidently a process to render the fungus (even) more palatable. *ius* is the origin of our modern culinary term 'jus': here the fig-peckers (**ficedulas**) are swimming 'in the same (i.e. mushroom) sauce'. The metaphor **natantes** (literally 'swimming') effectively evokes the birds in the liquid.

9 mergere continues the theme of **condire** and means 'to drown' – a meaning which has added piquancy as the young man 'drowns' the birds as they 'swim'. The fig-pecker (or beccafico) was a small bird served whole as a delicacy.

9–10 The 'useless parent and his white-haired gullet' is vivid language for 'the greedy wastrel old parent'. The word *nebulo* literally means 'fog-man' and is not uncommon in Roman vituperative language. The **gula** is the gullet or throat (cf. 15.90), used here for the appetite which fed it: here the imagery is a grotesque caricature as the gullet is 'white-haired' (**cana**, i.e. belonging to an old man) and is somehow 'demonstrating' the recipes. **monstrante** picks up **monstrant** from 3.

10–11 The 'seventh year' is the time when formal education usually began and acted as a dividing line between infancy and childhood in ancient societies which liked to divide life into seven-year periods. The poet here perhaps mentions teeth because they are of great importance to the child who is already a connoisseur of fine food: if so, **nondum omni** adds a hint of impatience as the child greedily awaits his new set of teeth.

12 At the age of seven a boy would normally be passed on to a professional teacher for elementary education. Teachers were paid by the parents: the hyperbole here of a 'thousand tutors' being brought in to re-educate the child continues the extravagance already evoked in the lavish food (as well as underlining how unteachable the child is). **barbatos** is more than a vivid epithet: wearing a beard was the mark of a Greek and/or a philosopher. Such tutors were often Greek slaves.

12–13 **mille** often indicates an unfeasibly large number: see *OLD* s.v. 'mille' 1b and cf. Catullus 5.7–10, 16.12, 35.8. **mille inde / hinc totidem** is a neat chiasmus, and the poet varies the language by saying **mille . . . totidem** rather than *mille . . . mille*. The words **inde** and **hinc**

totidem add little to the overall sense of the sentence but the extended phrasing suggests the protracted search for teachers.

13-14 *lautus* derives from *lavatus* ('washed') and is used of extravagant and wealthy people. *paratus* has the specialized sense here of 'the service of the dinner table'. **semper** is stressed in enjambement – the boy wishes to dine like this *all* the time and not just on feast days. **degenerare** (to 'decline from a standard') suggests the fastidious youth refusing to compromise on his *haute cuisine* (**magna ... culina**: *culina* literally means 'kitchen' but also by synecdoche it means the food prepared there).

23-4 Housman transposed these lines here to make the passage make better sense. The transposition also makes for effective ring-composition as the poet begins and ends this section (15–24) with gruesome details of pain inflicted on slaves.

23 The subject of the verb **suadet** is the **laetus** man whose tastes are listed in line 24 (**quem...carcer**). It is understood that he is the father of the young man (**iuveni**), as at 121 and 191. *stridor* is usually an unpleasant sound and the phrasing is aptly reminiscent of Virgil *Aeneid* 6.558 (*stridor ferri tractaeque catenae* ('the clanking of iron and chains dragged along')) where the damned are being tortured in the underworld and the noises cause Aeneas to be gripped with fear: the use of such well-known epic language is ironic in the case of this cruel philistine. The use of chains to punish slaves was common.

24 This line adds more detail to line 23. **afficiunt** here has the meaning 'excite' or 'move (emotionally)', and together with **mire** comes to mean 'stir with admiring emotion'. There is a breathless asyndetic list of slave-punishments: **inscripta** (passive participle of *inscribo*) means 'branded marks' such as were burnt onto the skin of slaves. The *ergastulum* was a place of punishment for slaves, from which they would emerge during the day to work, while **carcer** may denote little more than enclosed slave-accommodation. This slave-owner gets abundant aesthetic pleasure from these routine arrangements to prevent slaves from absconding.

15–22 In this long rhetorical question two types of slave-owner are contrasted: the 'enlightened' philosophical master who believes that slaves and free-born are all made from the same human material, and the sadistic master (whom we met in 23–4) now written up as a Homeric monster. Ancient attitudes towards slavery were varied, although few people questioned the need for slavery as an institution.

15 The idea of the **mitem animum** is helped by the mild 'm' alliteration. The language of this line is all positive: *aequus* means 'fair' or 'just' while *errores* are by definition 'mistakes' rather than overt vices – and these *errores* are only **modicis**.

16–17 ut . . . putet follows on from **praecipit**: the father instructs the boy 'to think that the souls . . .'. The ideas here are Stoic, albeit couched in Epicurean terminology – **materia** (originally 'timber') means 'the basic substance of the universe' and **elementis** is a common word for Epicurus' 'atoms' (e.g. Lucretius 2.393, 2.411). **nostrā** is ablative singular agreeing with **materiā**.

18 The philosophical curriculum extended over three counterfactual lines (15–17) is contrasted with the grim alternative in the single word **saevire**. The emphasis on 'teaching' is brought out by **docet**, picking up **praecipit** (16). **Rutilus** is not known but the name may be significant (cf. Fuscinus in line 1): as an adjective *rutilus* means 'glowing red' (cf. 299) and could well describe a red-faced regular user of hot irons (**ardenti ferro** 22). **gaudet acerbo** is a powerful oxymoron, and the line is framed by words of harshness.

19 The heavy spondaic rhythm of **plāgārum** evokes the rhythm of the beating and the line is framed with words of whipping.

A Level

19–20 The sadistic slave-owner is described using figures from Homer's *Odyssey*: the Sirens were the captivating bird-females whose voices lured sailors to their death (Homer *Odyssey* 12.39–46, 165–200), while Antiphates was the leader of the cannibalistic Laestrygonians (10.80–132) and Polyphemus was the (equally cannibalistic) Cyclops (9.105–566). The comparisons are well-made: the man considers the sound of the lash more attractive than the irresistible song of the Sirens, with the word **flagellis** having its own cruel resonance, while his focalized self-image as gigantic man-eating ogre is put into ironic context with the qualifying term **trepidi laris**: the *Lares* were the household gods and so (although the word is here synecdochic for 'household' (cf. 15.153, see *OCD* s.v. 'Lares')) the descriptive term **trepidi** suggests that his rage is enough to make even a god tremble. The final four-syllable name to end the line is not unusual in Juvenal (cf. 6.71, 6.110) and Homer also ends lines with this very name (*Odyssey* 9.407, 446). Tales from the *Odyssey* appear a good deal in Roman satire: cf. 15.13–26, 9.149–50, Horace *Sat.* 2.3.14 (Sirens), 1.5.63 (Cyclops): it is clear that Roman readers were expected to be familiar with the Greek tales.

21 This epic tormentor does not do the dirty work himself but hires a *tortor* for the purpose. **aliquis** is pointed: it does not matter who is suffering so long as 'somebody' is in pain: and **tunc** suggests that he is not happy unless this is going on.

22 The reason for the branding is trivial: **lintea** may refer to linen which the slave has allowed to be stolen at the baths (as at Petronius 30.7–11). For the burning of slaves with 'blazing iron' see 24n.

25–30 The speaker now turns to sexual immorality as learned behaviour, a topic he has already rehearsed at 6.231–41 (where the young wife has been schooled by her mother) and which is described also by Ovid (*Ars Amatoria* 3.611–66) and hinted at by Horace (*Odes* 3.6.21–4). The mother tells her daughter about her own lovers and also teaches her what to write in the love-letters which she (the daughter) now sends to *her* lover using the same **cinaedis** (go-betweens) as her mother does/did. In this instance it is a mother teaching her daughter (whereas in lines 4–24 it was fathers teaching sons).

25-6 **rusticus** ('of the countryside') came to be a pejorative term for unsophisticated and boorish behaviour in life and literature; it connotes a person who is naive in matters of sex at e.g. Ovid *Amores* 1.8.44, 3.4.37 ('anyone who is hurt when his wife is unfaithful is just too *rusticus*'). *Larga* is another significant name ('Mrs Free-with-her-favours').

26 A *moechus* is a man who commits adultery with a married woman: cf. 6.23–4n. The Greek word (as at line 30) has a strongly pejorative tone.

26-7 Two different terms describe the recitation: **dicere** ('to name') followed by the more interesting phrase **contexere cursu**. *contexo* is to 'weave together' (*con* + *texo*) and so here means to 'join together' in a sequence, while *cursus* (from *curro* ('I run')) has the sense of 'rapid speaking'. **tam cito** is picked up and amplified with **tanto . . . cursu** and the extension of the sentence runs the reader (along with the girl) out of breath. It may be relevant that running and weaving would be normal activities for a Roman girl.

28 **ter deciens** is ambiguous (meaning either 'thirty times' or 'thirteen times') and the poet is presumably happy to leave the meaning unclear with the possibility that the number of breaths could be as many as thirty. **respiret** here means 'take a breath'.

28-9 The closeness of the mother and daughter is brought out by the juxtaposition of the words **matri / virgo** in enjambement, and **conscia** denotes the guilt-by-association brought about by the girl

A
Level

being cognisant of her mother's misdeeds: for this word in this sexual
sense see 6.271.

29   The line sets up a temporal contrast: when she was unmarried
(**virgo**) the girl merely connived at what her mother was doing, whereas
now (**nunc**) that she is herself older she receives active instruction,
with **hac** referring to the mother. The wax tablets (**ceras**) are described
with the pathetic diminutive **pusillas** which makes obvious sense as
such love-notes would need to be concealed, but the diminutive also
suggests that the girl is herself not yet grown-up. **dictante** indicates
'dictating' words. Wax tablets made useful vehicles for notes (cf. 14.191)
especially love-letters (6.233, Ovid *Amores* 2.5.5) and had the advantage
of being able to be erased instantly upon reading.

30   The enthusiasm of the mother (and the girl) is brought out by
the verb **implet** (stressed in enjambement) which shows that she has
plenty to write. *cinaedus*, like *moechus*, is a Greek word (meaning
originally 'dancer') and conveys disgust, strengthened by the placing
of the two words in the same line.

31–3   The lines form an impressive rhetorical flourish: there is the
pompous statement (**sic natura iubet**) followed by the generalization
about 'us' which is enhanced by the pleonasm of **velocius et citius** and
the well-chosen word **auctoribus** (conveying both 'authority' and also
'parents') to end the sentence. There is a slight oxymoron in **domestica
magnis** which focalizes the picture to a child's-eye view (to which
parents are indeed 'large').

31   The anthropomorphic personification of **natura** as an authority
is not uncommon. The bumpy rhythm of the end of this line adds to
the effect of urgency in **velocius et citius**.

32   **corrumpunt** is stressed in enjambement and the juxtaposition
with **vitiorum** further enhances the idea of wickedness. *exemplum*

here means 'example' in the sense of 'role-model', as commonly in historical writings: elsewhere (14.120, 15.32) it means 'instance'.

33 subeant is often used of mental states 'coming upon' us (cf. 14.202), with a pejorative tinge of aggression as the word also means to 'attack' or 'invade'.

34–73: We can all be taught bad ways and children should be protected from bad behaviour and bad language. How can you later reprimand a son who is only copying your own bad behaviour? You make more effort to clean your house for your visitors than to clean your life for your children.

74–84

An analogy from nature, assuming that human children are reared in the same way as birds and also assuming that physiological feeding habits can be compared to psychological moral choices. The list is in ascending order of length of description: the stork (3 lines), the vulture (4 lines) and finally the eagle (5 lines).

74 The stork (**ciconia**) was seen as a model of parent-chick relations. The juxtaposed word order of **serpente ciconia pullos** is 'cinematographic' as we see the serpent next to the stork and then the stork next to her chicks.

75 per devia rura emphasizes the zeal of the bird in going to the middle of nowhere, and the goal of its long searching (**lacerta**) is revealed only at the end of the line.

76 sumptis pinnis reminds the Roman reader of the 'taking the toga' (*toga sumpta*) which indicates the formal entry of a young man into manhood when he assumes the toga.

77–8 The speaker now turns to the vulture. Carrion from cattle, dogs and dead criminals is disgusting (to us) but chicks reared on it will enjoy it.

A Level

77 The food is listed here in descending order of acceptability: cattle, then dogs, and finally human flesh – referred to with the grim metonymy of 'crosses' and enhanced with assonance and alliteration. **iumento** refers to beasts of burden such as mules, horses and oxen. Dogs are more often the eaters than the eaten (see e.g. Homer *Iliad* 1. 5–6, 24.211, Sophocles *Antigone* 206, Catullus 108.6) and only the most callous scavenger would eat a scavenger. Crosses were used to crucify those sentenced to death (see *OCD* s.v. 'crucifixion'): corpses of the crucified made a perfect ready-meal for the vulture.

78 **fetus** are the bird's chicks and there is a pleasing balance between the newly born and the newly dead (**cadaveris**), along with plosive alliteration and framing of the line with similar-sounding words (**ad fetus . . . affert**). Beautiful poetry is here created out of the ugliest of subject-matter.

79–80 The emphasis here is on **magni quoque** (i.e. 'also when it is (grown) big') and the increased size of the bird is suggested by the overspilling of the sentence into line 80 with the emphatic **se / pascentis**. **et** links the twin descriptive phrases **magni** and **se pascentis** (which both agree with **vulturis**).

80 The chick has fledged and now has its own (**propria**) tree for its own nest, the words **arbore nidos** juxtaposed in verse as in life. Vultures do not in fact nest in trees, but in rocks.

81–5 The poet does not name the eagle and makes use of epic language and allusion to identify it. Eagles are commonly regarded as the agents of Jupiter (e.g. Homer *Iliad* 24.311, Horace *Odes* 4.4.1, Virgil *Aeneid* 5.255, 9.564 (seizing a hare as here)) and so deserve the epithet **generosae**. The details here are reminiscent of epic similes such as Homer *Iliad* 22.308–11 (Hector swoops at Achilles 'like a high-flying eagle who moves towards the earth through the dark clouds to snatch either a tender lamb or a cowering hare'): cf. also Homer *Iliad* 15.690–4 and Virgil *Aeneid* 11.751–6.

A Level

81   The poet itemizes the prey before naming the predators.

82   **in saltu** contrasts with **per devia rura** in 75 and denotes the glades in which the eagle flies. The primary meaning of *cubile* is of a bed for human beings (as at 6.118) but the word is also used of the resting places of animals and birds.

83   **ponitur** (stressed in enjambement) is a term borrowed comically from *haute cuisine* ('served up') which creates a caricature of the parent bird waiting on their young. **se . . . levavit** here has a literal sense as the chicks will 'raise themselves up' when they have learned to fly.

84   **stimulante fame** is vivid language recalling the epic similes where a beast is driven on to kill by 'mad hunger' (e.g. Homer *Odyssey* 6.133, Virgil *Aeneid* 9.340, 10.724): and the harsh 'f' alliteration (**fame festinat**) adds further emphasis. The final vowel of **famē** is long (as at 6.424, 15.102, Virgil *Georgics* 4.318)

85   The poet repeats **praedam** from line 82, verbally enacting the repetitive feeding. **rupto gustaverat ovo** is well written: eating-habits are traced back to the very first taste (**gustaverat**) when the chick first left the egg.

86–95   Real estate in ancient Rome was scarce and the population-density was high for an ancient city: this meant that the ability to build large properties was a marker of extreme wealth and therefore attractive to the status-hungry. Builders in the city itself built ever higher (cf. **alta** 88), while the rich made sure that they also had coastal or suburban villas to which they could retreat. The locations of the three villas are interesting: *Caieta* (modern Gaita) is 173km from Rome, while *Tibur* (modern Tivoli) and *Praeneste* (modern Palestrina) are much closer (34km and 41km respectively). Tibur is 162km distant from Caieta – a journey which would have taken Caetronius about five days to make – and the juxtaposition of the two places in a single line (87) is sardonic, all the more because the buildings go from sea-level (**litore**) to hill (**summa ... arce**) in a few words.

86   **Caetronius** is unknown, although the name (and its variant Cetronius) was not uncommon. **aedificator** is a word only found here in Latin verse and seems to have had a hint of grandiosity.

86–7   Caieta was supposedly named after the nurse of Aeneas who died there (Virgil *Aeneid* 7.1–2). The haste with which the villas are created is brought out by the sequence of **modo ... nunc ... nunc**.

88–90   Praeneste (at 450m. above sea-level) was 'cool' (3.190, Horace *Odes* 3.4.22) and the spondaic rhythm of line 88 perhaps indicates the laborious climb up to the town: the theme of 'lofty' is conveyed in the adjective **alta** and also in the specification of **culmina** (literally 'roofs') as being the end-result aimed at – the term here both being synecdochic for 'buildings' while also keeping our eyes on their height. White marble of good quality was quarried in Etruria in Italy, but this builder imports *his* marble from Greece, presumably preferring the coloured forms which could be obtained from there (at much greater expense): transporting the materials over long distances (**longeque petitis**) was hugely expensive and the plural form of the noun (**marmoribus**) suggests the quantity being used.

90   **vincens** here has the sense of 'outstripping' in grandeur and perhaps in height: Caetronius creates his (superior) buildings next to existing ones. Praeneste was famous for its huge temple of *Fortuna Primigenia*, extending over 400 metres and rising 137 metres up the hill. Tibur had a sanctuary of Hercules Victor (dimension: 3000m^2) which housed a massive statue of the hero as well as a library. The order of temples is the reverse of the order of their locations as listed in lines 87–8: and there is a nice irony in this builder being superior both to Fortune and to Hercules – a superiority which is at once brought down to earth with the bathos of line 91.

A
Level

91   Posides was a wealthy freedman eunuch (**spado**): he was a favourite of the emperor Claudius (Suetonius *Claudius* 28) and built baths at Baiae as well as (apparently) a house near to the temple of Capitoline Jupiter. The line is a masterly sneer which undercuts the previous five lines in bathetic sarcasm: the appetite for building big is equated to that of a castrated freedman, and this foreign *parvenu* is clearly no match in fact for 'our' (**nostra**) Capitol, for all his efforts. The line is neatly constructed, being framed by the eunuch (**spado ... Posides**), juxtaposing him with the large structure of **Capitolia nostra** and conveying the effort involved with the heavy spondees and the imperfect tense of **vincebat**. **spado** is a highly pejorative term.

92–4   Caetronius spent massively on his building programme and yet (**tamen**) still left his heir enough to do the same: the son inherits the craze for building along with the remaining cash. The phrasing is balanced and rhetorical, with two staccato parallel clauses (**imminuit rem / fregit opes**) in asyndeton leading to a third longer phrase revealing the true extent of the inheritance.

92   dum here (as at 95) means 'since' rather than 'while' and *habito* is intransitive ('to be housed'). **imminuit rem**: the final monosyllable conveys the (relatively) tiny amount of the initial wealth left behind.

93   fregit (from *frango*) is a powerful verb to denote both 'breaking up' the wealth and also 'exhausting' it (cf. 14.161).

93–4   The litotes **nec parva** is appropriate here as we expect the legacy to be very small after the strong verbs **imminuit ... fregit** and so **nec ... tamen** is needed to correct this assumption. **mensura ... partis** here refers to the 'size of the share' of a legacy.

94–5   The vignette of Caetronius ends with a superb caricature of the crazy (**amens**) son as he 'raises up' new villas made with 'better marble'. **totam hanc** assumes *partem*. The father broke up (**fregit**) his wealth, and the son duly 'frittered away' (**turbavit**) *his* share.

95 Note the detail of the marble as the mark of the superior villa (see 88–90n.) and the juxtaposition of key attributes (**meliore novas**) for effect. The instantaneous present tense verb **attollit** makes the process look quick and easy.

96–106

The speaker now turns to Jewish families for more evidence of parental influence. Jews feature in Roman satire (3.14, 3.296, Horace *Satires* 1.5.100, 1.9.68–71, Persius 5. 179–84) as a fairly easy target because of their distinctive beliefs and practices: marked antisemitism is shown here, in line with the satirist's cynical tendency always to impute base motives for human behaviour.

96 It is assumed that readers will understand the term **Sabbata**: elsewhere Juvenal glosses the term as 'the seventh day' (see 105 below: cf. also 6.159–60). The words **metuentem** (literally 'fearing') and **metuunt** (at 101) need to be taken in the sense of 'reverent towards' or 'feeling respect for'.

97 Jews were in Roman eyes 'atheists' as they paid no respect to Roman deities, being forbidden to make images of God or even to use the name of God. Jews sometimes substituted the word for 'sky' for 'God' which lies perhaps behind **caeli numen** here: the supreme god for Romans was the sky-god Jupiter, but the speaker satirizes their belief with mention of 'clouds' (**nubes**) which recalls the highly atypical deities of Aristophanes' comedy *Clouds*.

98 Tacitus (*Histories* 5.4) ascribes the Jewish refusal to eat pork to a fear of catching the skin-disease suffered by pigs, and the injunction is turned here into the comic trope that they regard pig-flesh as no more

A Level

palatable than human flesh. The faint hint of cannibalism conveyed in the juxtaposition of **humana carne suillam** is going to be magnified in the very different Egyptian setting of *Satire* 15. Pork was the commonest form of meat in ancient Rome, where peasants kept pigs (*OCD* s.v. 'food and drink'), where cows were working animals and where sheep and goats were too useful for milk and wool to be eaten. *suillus* is the adjective from *sus* ('pig') and here understands the word *carnem*.

99–100 Circumcision as a Jewish ritual is an easy target: **mox** ('after that') and the active verb **ponunt** suggest that the sons – not content with the weaker form of their parents' Judaism – become fully-fledged Jews of their own accord, even voluntarily undergoing circumcision. The plosive alliteration in the line comically imitates the snipping.

101 The speaker here mimics biblical language in his string of three main verbs – a device known as 'parataxis' – framed by the all-encompassing **Iudaicum . . . ius**. The final monosyllable gives the line a syncopated rhythm. The three verbs denote a sequence of piety: being inducted into the knowledge of the faith (**ediscunt**), keeping it in their lives (**servant**) and then maintaining reverence (**metuunt**).

102 **quodcumque** suggests an uncritical attitude on the part of the Jews: **arcano . . . volumine** refers to the Pentateuch (the first five books of the Hebrew Bible) which was written on a single scroll (*volumen*) and was attributed to Moses (**Moyses**) who led the Jewish people out of slavery in Egypt to their 'promised land' in Palestine. **arcano** (literally 'secret') here means 'mystic': there may also be a play on the word *arca* ('wooden chest') as the *volumen* was stored in such a vessel.

103–4 Jewish exclusiveness is here described as contrary to common humanity and ancient traditions of guest-friendship. The words may also perhaps have metaphorical force: 'showing the way' (**monstrare vias**) meaning 'granting access' to people seeking to share the Jewish wisdom if they will take the necessary steps (e.g. circumcision), and the **fontem** may be an allusion to washing rituals. **eadem** goes with **sacra**, and the infinitives (**monstrare** and **deducere**) are explanatory of **ius** in 101.

104 The heavy spondees of the line creates a sense of struggle as the strangers seek the water – only for the line to end with the bathetic word **verpos**. *verpus* (the adjectival form of the offensive noun *verpa*) indicates a state in which the glans of the penis is exposed either due to arousal or (as here) circumcision.

105 **in causa [esse]** means 'to be responsible'.

105–6 The weekly sabbath is said not to 'touch any part of their lives' in the sense that Jews did not carry on any of their normal activities that day. The alleged laziness (**ignava**) this represented is evoked with sluggish spondees.

107–37 The argument moves to the hoarding of money with no intention of spending it.

107–8 The juxtaposition of **cetera solam** marks a strong contrast and introduces avarice as being unique (**solam**), with contrast of the willing (**sponte**) and the unwilling (**inviti**): the element of 'force' is brought out by the terms **inviti . . . iubentur** framing line 108. The two verbs are also contrasted: the spontaneous **imitantur** and the coerced **iubentur**. **quoque** goes with **inviti** – 'even against their will'. Line 108 is metrically awkward, having no caesura in the third or the fourth foot.

109 Avarice is a **vitium** but it can look like (**specie**) a good quality such as prudence or being thrifty (*parcus*). The superficial similarity of a vice and a virtue is made all the more effective by the juxtaposition of **vitium specie virtutis** and by the additional gloss **umbra** which here means 'semblance' but whose meanings also include 'ghost' and 'shade' – meanness is thus the 'dark side' of thrift.

110   A thumbnail sketch of the miser, with vivid details of his appearance. *habitus* here refers to 'clothing', leaving this line with a balanced A-B-A form of clothing – face – clothing. **cum** here means 'since': the appearance explains how the mean man reaps praise.

111–13   **frugi** (formed as the predicative dative from *frux*) functions as an indeclinable adjective meaning 'sensible, honest' and is a euphemism for 'mean'. The comparison and contrast of **frugi** and **avarus** is enhanced by the word-order and the word **laudetur** also raises the stakes even higher as he is not merely tolerated but positively 'praised', and the praise is awarded with no hesitation (**nec dubie**). The positive terms accumulate, with effective anaphora of **tamquam** leading to the climactic **magis quam** as the miser is elevated to the status of a mythical beast. The subjunctives **laudetur** and **servet** go with **cum** in 110 and continue the explanation of the miser's virtuous image.

113–14   Two famous mythical guards: the *Hesperides* ('daughters of Evening') were said to live in the far West, near the Atlas mountains, where they nurtured a tree which grew golden apples and which had been a wedding present from the goddess Earth to Juno when she married Jupiter. The dragon which guarded the place was called Ladon and one of the labours of Hercules was to steal these golden apples. **Ponticus** ('of the Black Sea') refers to Colchis (in what is now Western Georgia on the shores of the Black Sea) where a dragon guarded the golden fleece which belonged to the winged ram which carried Phrixus and Helle over the sea to escape their stepmother Ino. The quest of this golden fleece was the object of the voyage of the Argo under its captain Jason, who duly acquired it with the magical assistance of the witch Medea. The adjective **Ponticus** alone is sufficient to identify the dragon guarding the golden fleece: the poet assumes a level of mythological knowledge in his readership born (no doubt) of the same recycling of mythical tales which he bemoans at

A
Level

1.1–13. The point of comparison in both cases here is the gold which both the dragons and the miser are guarding.

114–16 After the lofty epic comparison the poet lowers his poetic register with a highly prosaic sentence. 114 has a marked bucolic diaeresis (pause before the fifth foot of the hexameter) followed by a string of short words (and final monosyllable), leading in enjambement to another line with bucolic diairesis and a heavy fifth foot spondee (**ācquīr / ēndī**) which leads in turn to the emphatic enjambed word **artificem. adde quod** is a didactic phrase: cf. 15.47. The effect is one of studied inelegance, belied by the plosive alliteration of **populus putat**, the key word **egregium** (derived from *grex* (a herd or flock) and so nicely apt after mention of the golden fleece) and above all the final description of **acquirendi/ artificem** which is a wonderful paradox of the prosaic and the aesthetic, as the word *artifex* commonly denotes artistic and technical creativity: the pretentiously artistic emperor Nero is said (Suetonius *Nero* 49.1) to have said before his death *qualis artifex pereo* ('O what an artist dies with me!').

116–18 **artificem** leads on to the caricature of the miser as one who can somehow create the precious metals he craves by the unstinting use of the anvil (**incude**) and the forge (**camino**). The poet moves from a singular miser (**hunc** 114) to the plural (**his ... fabris**). **his fabris** is either ablative absolute ('with these men acting as blacksmiths') or else dative of advantage (the fortunes grow 'for these blacksmiths').

117 This line adds to the force of 118 if one understands it as meaning '[fortunes] grow and become greater by any means possible, provided that the men use the anvil constantly and keep the forge always blazing'. The repetition of **crescunt** suggests the obsessive quest for financial growth.

118 The line is neatly framed with the key metallurgical terms **incude** and **camino**. The juxtaposition of the two words denoting

'unceasing' (**assidua semperque**) is also powerful, as is the 'd' and 'c'
alliteration in the line suggestive of the hammering.

119 The previous sentence had described the opinion of the *populus*:
now we see also (**et**) the figure of the father. *felix* has the meaning of
'happy' unlike *beatus* which has strong overtones of 'fortunate' in material
circumstances (see next line). **animi felices** means 'happy in mind'.

120–1 The anaphora of **qui . . . qui** introduces two parallel relative
clauses which show the fetishizing of wealth from two different points
of view: the positive ('wealth is admirable') and the negative ('the
poor cannot be happy'). **beati / pauperis** is (for this miser) an
oxymoron as *beatus* (for him) means 'wealthy'.

122 Two images of wealth-seeking are powerfully combined here:
that of a 'path' (**via**) to be followed and that of a 'code of behaviour'
(**sectae**), with the two images joined with the parallel demonstratives
illa and **eidem**. *secta* (from *sequor* ('I follow')) has the primary
meaning of 'a course along which one travels' and (with **via**) frames
the line with words denoting travel. **incumbere** (literally to 'lean on')
here has the sense of 'to devote one's energies to'.

123 **elementa** denotes both the 'rudiments' to be taught to children
(as in Horace *Satires* 1.1.26, *Epistles* 1.20.17) and also the letters of the
alphabet which make up words (cf. Lucretius 1. 907–14), and both
meanings well suit the education of the young in vices.

123–4 This parent wastes no time. **elementa** suggests early
childhood (see previous note), **protinus** states that this starts 'at once'
and **imbuit** is a strong verb of induction, gaining in power by being
coupled with **cogit**. **sordes** is left to the end of the line for maximum
effect and is strongly pejorative: meaning essentially physical 'dirt', it
came to mean 'squalid' and thus suggests 'mean' or 'avaricious' as such
people would prefer to be squalid than to spend money. **sordes** as a

**A
Level**

---

subject on the child's curriculum (for him to 'master' (**ediscere**)) is a provocative image and the qualifying term **minimas** gives the pupil the 'child's portion' amount of **sordes** appropriate to his age.

124–5 The child next (**mox**) graduates to limitless greed, and the interchange of learning (**ediscere**) and teaching (**docet**) is well put. **votum** properly denotes an oath accompanied by a promise to the deity, although here it means little more than 'heart's desire' as at 6.60.

126 A *modius* was a container used to measure out corn (containing about eight-and-a-half litres): the word **iniquo** here means 'delivering short-measure'. The hungry slaves are depicted with sluggish spondees (**sērvōrūm vēntrēs**) suggestive of their famished feebleness. **castigat** normally denotes the correction of crimes or immoral acts but here the slaves' only offence is to need feeding.

127 This master also goes hungry (**esuriens**) which distinguishes this scene (like Horace *Satires* 1.1.94–9) from those places (such as Juvenal *Satire* 5) where the rich eat lavishly while the slaves or clients suffer. What could be classed as a virtue ('thrift') becomes a vice when taken to excess and when indulged in from selfish motives: see 109n. above.

127–8 The hungry master still cannot bear (**sustinet**: cf. 15.88) to eat up all (**omnia**) the crusts. The description of the food makes the reader assume that this is because they are inedible, but the speaker springs the surprise that he saves some up for later when they will be even *more* mouldy. The juxtaposition of **mucida caerulei** emphasizes the disgust: *mucidus* has the primary sense of 'snotty' (cf. 'mucus') but here means 'mouldy'; *caeruleus* ('blue') shows the distinctive blue-white *penicillium* mould found on old bread.

129 The line is framed by **hesternum ... minutal. minutal** was minced food: the word (like the English word 'mince') is derived from *minutus* ('small') and so means a dish 'consisting of fine pieces', suggesting that even small scraps are being treated in this way (cf. **minimas** at 124), let alone larger chunks of meat. Here the miser makes a habit (**solitus**) of 'keeping safe' (**servare**) old food in the middle of September.

130-1 Autumn was notorious for fevers and ill-health. Hoarding stale and mouldy food is a squalid practice but elegant epic language is used to focalize the value of these scraps to the miser. **nec non** began as a colloquialism but became an elevated way of saying 'and' in Virgil and his successors: it is used for mock-epic grandeur here. The enjambement of **cenae / alterius** is effective as it enacts the waiting time between the two dinners. **alterius** here means 'another' or 'a second [meal]' as at 141 below. **conchem** refers to a type of bean and is the poor man's food (see 3.293, 11.58, Horace *Satires* 2.6.63). The adjective **aestivam** ('summery') here means 'in summer'.

131-2 **parte** and **dimidio** indicate that he is saving up what has not been eaten in the first dinner. **lacerti** (the Atlantic Chub Mackerel (*Scomber colias*)) was a common fish but not the cheapest – which may help to explain why leftovers are precious. **signatam** here means 'locked up': the term derives from the seal (*signum*) which was used to protect a letter from being read by others, but the seal is here applied to protect the leftovers from the hungry (126) slaves. **siluro** refers to the European catfish or sheatfish.

133 **includere** continues the idea of locking up from **signatam**, while **numerata** adds an extra touch of suspicion in that this master will 'count' them in case somebody gains access to the safe place where they are locked up. The key defining term **porri** is left to the end of the line and the sentence for bathetic effect – all this effort for portions of a leek.

134 **aliquis de ponte** alludes to a beggar, as beggars would routinely sit by bridges where traffic would be forced to slow down and linger. The sentence ends with the forceful future indicative asserting that even a beggar 'will refuse' (**negabit**) this meal.

A
Level

135 **quo** here means 'to what purpose?' as at 15.61: we have to understand something like *quo [prodest habere] divitias . . .* The phrase **tormenta coactas** is a stark juxtaposition reinforcing the idea that wealth is only obtained through suffering: **tormenta** are properly 'tortures', but the word is metaphorical here ('torment').

136 An elegant line, with two different words for 'madness' at both ends and two forms of 'obvious' in-between, the two phrases both introduced with **cum** both at the start of the line and after the caesura. **furor** and **phrenesis** both mean 'madness' but the terms are very different. **furor** commonly attaches to a feeling which is irrational and/or passionate – it indicates full-blown madness at 14.284, furious rage at 15.36, and furious hunger at 15.100. **phrenesis** derives from Greek and means 'inflammation of the brain' and is more of a medical term: the Greek term for this condition was generally used in Rome, presumably because the leading exponents of medicine were Greeks.

137 **ut** here introduces a purpose clause explaining why the miser (who has the means to live comfortably) chooses instead to live like a pauper. The key words are well balanced in the two halves of the line: rich (**locuples**) is opposed to poor (**egentis**), and death (**moriaris**) opposed to life (**vivere**). **fato** (literally 'fate' or 'death') nicely balances **moriaris** (and the juxtaposition **vivere fato** is close to saying that the austere life is a living death) and here has to be understood in the sense of 'the lifestyle which fortune gives you' as at 14.158.

138–40 There is an exponential growth in greed: the more money is made, the greater the desire for it, while the reverse is also true in that people without money stop seeking it.

138 The **sacculus** ('purse') would be carried out of the house, as distinct from the *ferrata arca* ('iron-clad safe'), in which the family savings were kept in the *atrium* of the house. The diminutive ending

-ulus (cf. Catullus 13.8) indicates both the affection in which the purse is held and also its smaller size: filling the **sacculus** is only the first stage of wealth-creation and it is tempting to imagine that its owner is still only a youth. The juxtaposition of words indicating 'full' (**pleno ... turget**) is effective, as is the metaphor **ore** (literally 'mouth') suggesting the imagery of greed as an urge to devour money.

139 A neat aphorism: the framing of the line with **crescit ... crevit** creates a chiasmus of **crescit amor ... pecunia crevit**.

140 The thinking – that if indulgence increases desire, then austerity will reduce it – is perhaps wishful and is the inverse of the principle outlined in line 139. Poor people may still wish for wealth but be resigned to never having any and so may appear to lack the desire for it. **hanc** must refer to **pecunia** from 139.

140–4 The avaricious man buys properties one after another: the style is suitably paratactic with a sequence of present indicative verbs (**paratur ... sufficit ... libet ... videtur ... mercaris**) to indicate the succession of ongoing purchases. The whole long sentence is directed at the addressee in the second person (**tibi**).

140–1 **paratur / altera** makes good use of enjambement to enhance the effect of adding property to property, and the increased portfolio is verbally enacted in the adding of **altera villa** to the single **rus ... unum**. Line 141 is neatly framed with the stressed words **altera ... unum**. The singular word **rus** means 'country estate' as at 6.55 and 14.155.

142–3 Envy is now added to the greed: the man 'wants' (**libet**) to advance (**proferre**) his 'territory', and the crop of his neighbour 'looks' (**videtur**) bigger and better (**maior ... et melior**) than his own.

143–4 The ending of 143 with its string of three monosyllables is suggestive of the breathless haste with which the purchases are made. The lavish description in line 144 almost sounds like the purchaser

**A
Level**

justifying his purchases with sales-patter: not just **arbusta** (a vineyard formed from growing vines up trees) but also a whole mountain (**montem**) which is coloured grey-green (**canet**) with the thick (**densa**) olives growing on it. The purchaser is investing in cash-crops (vines and olives) which would give him a good return. The poet might equally well have written *montem densa*: perhaps he wished to have **densa** looking back to **arbusta** as well as forward to **oliva** (with which it agrees): the placing of **montem** just after the caesura also throws emphasis onto it.

145–9 The greedy landowner vandalizes the neighbour's field to harass him into selling it, a form of bullying which was declared a crime in the early Roman legal code known as the 'Twelve Tables'. Here, the sequence of events is enhanced by the variation of tenses: **vincitur** is a vivid present tense and precedes the sending of the cattle which therefore goes into a threatening future tense (**mittentur**), which shows how the intention or threat to vandalize the land could be (but is not) enough to sway the reluctant seller.

145 The so-called 'master' (**dominus**) is not won over by 'any' (**ullo**) amount of money, and the power-struggle between the two men is brought out by the juxtaposition of **dominus non vincitur**. **quorum** goes with **dominus** and refers to the property listed in 144.

146–7 The cattle create a stampede of starving beasts, brought out by the listing of them as first **boves** and then pack animals (**iumenta**): their common characteristic is hunger, stressed both implicitly (**macri** – they are 'thin' for a reason) and then explicitly (**famelica**). Their hunger is born of hard work, as **lasso . . . collo** makes clear. The animals will be sent to wreck the corn (**aristas**) while it is green (**virides**) – that is, before it has had any time to make its owner any money.

148–9 The threat is carried out, with the cattle ravaging like 'scythes' (**falcibus**). They do not go home (**nec prius ... domum**) until the destruction is complete, as stressed by **tota** ('all of it') and also **saevos** ('raging') applied to **ventres** ('bellies'). We have to supply a verb such as *abibunt* with **domum**: the ellipsis here amounts to a syllepsis as **abeant** does double duty – the cattle do not 'depart' until the corn has 'departed' (into their stomachs). Hunger here has the power to turn what are usually tame beasts into wild ones, with the epithet **saevos** transferred from the ruthless neighbours to the stomachs of their animals. **novalia** (the plural of *novale*) means 'fields'. The second-person verbs **credas** and **possis** (in the next line) are addressed to the avaricious man. **actum** has to be understood as 'job done' leaving the emphasis to be on **falcibus**.

150-1   **quam multi** and **quot** mean much the same thing and line 151 extends and elaborates on line 150, which ends with the powerful emotional verb **plorent**: cf. 6.86, 6.272. **iniuria** here denotes 'wrongdoing' in general and **fecerit** means 'rendered'.

152   Such behaviour will incur public disgrace. **bucina** (an epic term for the trumpet or horn) is here used as a metaphor for the 'blare' of gossip, enacted in this line with its lack of any verb, with the loose syntax and harsh 'f' alliteration of **foede . . . famae** and the anaphora of **qui . . . quam** across the caesura. **sermones** essentially means simply 'conversation' or 'common gossip': it is also striking that Horace's satirical poems are entitled *sermones* which raises the possibility that the word here is ironic as it could even describe the poem we are now reading, especially since greed is such a common theme in satire. **qui** here is the interrogative adjective ('what **sermones**!').

153-5   The man addressed retorts (**inquit**) that he cares nothing for his reputation. The Latin here amounts to saying 'I would not give a fig for the praise of others if it meant living a poor life'.

153   The lupin was proverbially worthless and was even used on the stage as fake money. *tunica* (literally 'tunic') here means the 'pod' of the lupin containing the seeds. The final syllable of *malŏ* is short (cf. *praestŏ* in 212).

154 The choice of words is interesting. **vicinia** (the immediate 'neighbourhood' picking up *vicina* from 143) is neatly sandwiched within **toto . . . pago** ('the whole country district') in verse as in life.

155 **secantem** agrees with **me** in 154 and the miser derides the idea of him 'cutting the pathetic grain of a tiny estate'. The emphasis here is on the smallness (**exigui . . . paucissima**) and the poor quality (**farra**) of the yield. *far* was often used for plain food, and the tedium of the fare is brought out by the repetitious assonance of 'i' and later 'a' in this line. Moralists had long praised the virtues of the simple life but this avaricious man does not share their ideals.

156–60 The poet's tone in this long sentence is one of scathing sarcasm as he points out that all the wealth in the world will not secure health and happiness. The sentence is framed in a strong future conditional clause with future tenses (**carebis** etc) in the apodosis and the future perfect (**possederis**) in the protasis.

156–7 The scorn is at once apparent in the ironic **scilicet** and the jingle of **morbīs . . . carebīs**. The poet's tone is hectoring as he piles up four forms of pain in two pairs, denoting bodily suffering (**morbis et debilitate**) and then mental anguish (**luctum et curam**), with each pair having its own assertive future tense verb (**carebis . . . effugies**).

157–8 The third element of the man's future is that of longevity, with the notion of extended time enacted in the enjambed **tempora vitae / longa**. Juvenal has already told us (10.358) that long life is 'among the least of life's gifts', and so mere time is worthless unless it is accompanied by **fato meliore** as here.

159 **solus** is pointed ('in sole ownership') – in contrast to the ownership of the whole **populus Romanus** in 160 – and perhaps sardonic as it also reminds us of the social isolation which his avarice will cause. **tantum** is correlative with **quantum** in 160 ('so much land ... as') and **culti ... agri** is a partitive genitive going with **tantum**.

160 Titus Tatius was king of the Sabines when his people joined together with the Romans under Romulus. The final word **arabat** adds a touch of agricultural vividness to the vignette.

161-6 **mox** denotes the period after Titus Tatius, when a mere couple of acres was enough to reward men who had suffered a great deal for the state.

161 **fractis aetate** stresses the length of active service before they are allowed to retire: **fractis** is in the dative case as the indirect object of **dabantur** in 163.

161-2 The plosive 'p' alliteration and the enjambement make this an expressive phrase. The three Punic wars were fought between Rome and Carthage between 264 and 146 BCE. Pyrrhus (319–272 BCE), king of Epirus, fought against Rome from 280–275 BCE and here is elevated with the focalized term **immanem** ('brutal' but also 'massive' and 'monstrous'), while the threatening violence of the Molossians is indicated in synecdoche by drawing attention to their swords (**gladios**). The Molossians were the only people in Epirus to declare for Macedon in the wars between Rome and Macedon and their homeland was sacked by the Romans in 167 BCE, with 150,000 captives being taken. Pyrrhus was the most famous Molossian king, who defeated the Roman forces at Heraclea in 280 BCE and Ausculum in 279 BCE.

163 These men have endured the whole succession of conflicts (outlined in 161–2) and their reward is long awaited (**tandem**): there is contrast between the many injuries sustained and the few acres given as their reward. The Roman *iugerum* amounted to about two-thirds of an acre (0.27 hectares); two of these therefore amounted to a plot measuring one-and-a-third acres. The poverty is made even worse by adding the word **vix** ('barely') suggesting that some might not even get two **iugera**. Once again, the speaker seems to be praising the past (as contrasted with the corrupt present) and there is clearly an ironic tone to the fulsome language.

164   **vulneribus** is emphasized in enjambement to highlight the physical cost of military service – a point reinforced with mention of 'blood and toil' (**sanguinis atque laboris**).

165–6   **nulli** is the dative of *nullus* and is taken with **visa** (*est*) to mean: 'seemed to nobody'. **meritis minor** go together ('less than they deserved'). **ingratae / curta fides patriae** is elegantly composed, with **curta fides** (literally 'incomplete loyalty') meaning 'a lack of loyalty', framed by the pejorative term **ingratae** and then the climactically emotive word **patriae**.

166–71   This tiny plot of land fed a family whose size grows absurdly from line to line, building up to the bathetic climax of line 172.

166   The juxtaposition of the strong term **saturabat** and the diminutive **glebula** ('a little lump of earth') brings out the paradox that this undersized plot provides more than enough for them.

167   The catalogue of family members begins with the *paterfamilias* and then sets up the theme of 'crowded accommodation' with the neat oxymoron **turbamque casae** – a *turba* ought not to be able to fit into a *casa*.

167–9   Lines 167 and 168 both begin with a key family member (**patrem . . . uxor**). The wife is one who continues to produce children (**feta**), with a pleasing tableau of her in her pregnant stillness alongside the four playing children. The poet rattles off cardinal numbers in quick succession (**quattuor unus ... tres**): three of the four children are legitimate offspring and so are masters (**domini**) while the fourth is a slave-child. **vernula** is the diminutive of *verna* – the diminutive appropriate for an infant slave. A *verna* was any child born to a slave mother and was a slave, no matter who the father was. The presence of any slaves in this tiny poor cottage is perhaps implausible but adds to the vignette of the crowded house.

169–71 The *casa* already contains six people with another on the way: now older offspring are introduced to fill yet more space and eat more food, as hard work builds up large appetites. The agricultural work undertaken is stressed with the alliterative phrase **a scrobe vel sulco** ('from the ditch or the furrow'). *scrobis* probably indicates a ditch for the planting of trees and shrubs, whereas a *sulcus* is a furrow created by a plough for the sowing of crops (cf. 14.241 and 6.107). **altera cena / amplior** shows the success of their labour, producing a second (**altera**) and larger (**amplior**) daily meal.

171 The emphasis is on the quantity of this second meal, which takes up the whole line: **amplior ... grandes** as well as the use of the plural **pultibus**. *puls* was a sort of porridge and was a byword for humble food.

172 The poet rounds off this section of his poem with a generalization contrasting the glorious past with the degenerate present. **modus** means 'a measured amount' and **agri** is a partitive genitive going with it. The final word of the line is climactic: the plot which could once feed a family of (at least) eight is no longer enough even for a recreational garden.

173–4 The speaker returns to the main theme of the dangers of avarice. He begins with a broad generalization that avarice causes more crime than other vices, giving two examples of violent crime involving poison (**venena**) and a blade (**ferro**). These two methods of murder are both premeditated (the killer 'has mixed' (**miscuit**) the poison ready for use, while the mugger goes out on the streets (**grassatur**) with his knife). Understand *sunt* with **scelerum causae**.

175-6 This **cupido** is **saeva** as it involves violence. **census** is the term for 'personal wealth' as opposed to *patrimonium* (inherited wealth or estate), used (cf. 6.362, 14.227) to connote status as well as simple cash. **immodici** ('having no *modus*') picks up *modus* from 172 and is often used of excessive desire and unrestrained behaviour.

176-7 The next generalisation is couched in chiastic form (**fieri vult ... vult fieri**) with emphasis on **et cito** in the middle of the phrase. Juvenal's avaricious man adds impatience to his already impressive catalogue of character flaws.

177-8 The indignation is expressed in the polyptoton of **quae ... quis** introducing a pair of rising rhetorical questions. The objective genitive **legum** is joined to **reverentia** ('respect for the laws') whereas **properantis avari** is a possessive genitive meaning 'in the case of a miser in a hurry'. **pudor** denotes both 'shame' and 'decency': it ties neatly with **metus** as two reasons for respecting the laws – fear of being punished and anticipation of the shame of being called out.

179-88 The speaker now dramatizes traditional attitudes, choosing as his mouthpiece some anonymous members of the Marsi, Hernici and Vestini – ancient Italian tribes chosen to represent the hardy ways of old. The superannuated nature of the advice is emphasized by **olim** (suggesting that even the quotation is from the past) and **senex** (showing that the man in question is himself old).

179-80 The speech opens without introduction with a strong imperative addressed to young men (**o pueri**). The line is remarkable for 'c' alliteration and the joining together of the diminutive **casulis**

(from *casa* – 'small cottages', as if a *casa* were not already small enough) and the **collibus** which are the home of other innocent rustics at 6.296.

180 The Marsi and the Vestini were amongst the tribes who fought against Rome in the Social War of 91–87 BCE (and were only won over by being granted citizenship), while the Hernici fought against Rome in 306 BCE. Naming the three tribes makes for an accumulation of unanimous authority for the sentiments uttered, combining frugality, religious observance and morality with a rugged physical toughness which disdains luxury.

181–2 The verb **quaeramus** is a first person plural jussive subjunctive. The emphases here are on hard work – the bread is to be obtained by the plough (**aratro**) and not by purchase – and on frugality – what is 'enough' (**satis**) and no more.

182 The term **numina ruris** ('gods of the countryside') here refers to the rural divinities who control fertility and harvest, such as the gods of wine (*Liber*) and corn (*Ceres*: see note on 218–19). The gods positively praise (**laudant**) the deployment of laborious agriculture which is their gift (**munus**).

183 The language of **ope et auxilio** ('aid and assistance') with its almost tautological repetition suggests the tone of religious ritual. **gratae . . . munus** combines an expression of thanks to the gods with the point that corn tastes better than acorns.

184 *contingere* (+ dative) has the meaning 'to be granted to one' (as at 6.49), which is appropriate as the speaker sees the human ability to scorn acorns as the gift of the gods rather than a sign of human progress. **fastidia** well expresses feelings of repugnance and disdain: cf. 14.201. **quercus** literally means 'oak' but here denotes by synecdoche the acorns which the tree produced. Early man is often described as living on a diet of acorns (see 6.10): note how **veteris** makes the points both that this had been their food from olden times and also that they stored them up with frugal thrift.

185–8 A man who is content with little, who is not embarrassed (**pudet**) by his rough clothes, has no need to commit crimes and so will not want (**volet**) to have a criminal record. The perfect infinitive **fecisse** here has the force of 'to be guilty of having done'. The passage elevates the moral value of poverty (as at 6.294–5) but also paints a picture of the rustic (who can rebuff strong winds simply by his clothing) as stronger than his effete urban peers.

185–6 The *pēro* was a rough thick boot. The juxtaposition of **glaciem perone** strengthens the case as footwear which is elegant would be no good in icy conditions: this man has no shame (**non pudet**) so long as the footwear keeps out the cold.

186–7 **pellibus inversis** means that the animal skins have been reversed so that the furry side is worn close to the body.

187–8 The speaker delays naming the subject of this phrase until the last possible moment for maximum emphasis. He frames the crimes (**scelus atque nefas**) with their cause, with the adjectives (**peregrina ignotaque**) separated in hyperbaton from their noun (**purpura**). **quaecumque est** is a dismissive qualification ('whatever it is') which continues the theme of 'foreign and unknown to us' by suggesting that the speaker has not seen it, while **scelus atque nefas** denote the breaking of human and divine law respectively.

189–207 The rustic paternal advice of 179–88 is now replaced with their urban equivalent, with a vignette of a father waking his son from sleep to nag him into seeking material success.

189 We need to supply a verb such as *dabant* to this line. **veteres** does double duty, signifying both 'old (men)' (cf. **senex** in 181), and also 'men of past times' as contrasted with people now (**nunc**).

minoribus (the comparative of *parvus*) means 'younger people' or more specifically 'their descendants'.

190   After autumn ends, the nights become longer and so working hours have to be extended into the hours of darkness: **media de nocte** may be a neat focalization as what is (in winter) early morning will seem to the comatose youth to be the middle of the night.

191   The word order is expressive: after the darkness and the slumber of the previous line, the **clamosus ... pater** verbally envelops the **iuvenem** with the awakening (**excitat**) placed last in the phrase as the shouting takes effect.

191–3   The father fires out six imperatives in less than three lines, and the string of shorter words in 192 effectively shows him barking his commands with heavy speech accents.

191   ceras (literally 'wax') refers to wooden tablets with a surface layer of wax on one side which could be erased and re-used *ad infinitum* (see 14.29).

192   The sequence is interesting: 'write' (**scribe**) and 'do not go back to sleep' (**vigila**), reminding us that it is night-time and the addressee is a teenager (**puer**). *causas agere* (usually meaning 'to plead a case in court') here refers to the preparation of cases rather than their actual delivery.

192–3   Roman law had a long history (see *OCD* s.v. 'law and procedure, Roman') going back to the 'Twelve Tables' of 450 BCE. These ancestral laws were **rubras** ('red-lettered') because the chapter-headings were routinely written in red: the heavy spondees of **maiorum leges** evokes the majesty of the law.

193   Military service is held out as an alternative to a legal career, the youth being told to apply for it in writing (**libello**). The vine staff (**vitem**) was the symbol of a centurion's authority. Young Romans from the senatorial and equestrian classes would expect to do some military service before entering civil careers, but the youth here is seen as one who will stay in the army until his sixtieth year, which suggests that he was from a lower class and that his ultimate aim was to become a senior centurion (*primipilaris*).

194–5   Laelius must be the commanding officer who will (the father hopes) admire his son's rough physique. The key features here are a lack of concern over personal appearance, maturity and obvious strength. Combing one's hair might not seem to indicate dandyish foppery, but having a 'head untouched by a comb' and 'shaggy nostrils' both suggest that the young man is hardy and unsullied by urban sophistication – and so better able to withstand the rigours of camp life than his soft urban contemporaries. Excessive concern with one's appearance is often criticized: see e.g. 2.99 where the emperor Otho is abused for carrying a mirror in his kit. **alas** is well chosen: the word commonly has a military meaning ('wing of an army' or 'unit of troops') as well as its primary anatomical sense here ('upper arm' or 'shoulder') and the general will see the lad in military as well as physiological terms.

196   *Mauri* are the Moors of Mauretania in North Africa, while the Brigantes were the largest and the most infamous tribe in Britain (see Tacitus *Agricola* 31.4). The choice of these names indicates that the youth is to cross the whole Roman empire. The line is neatly phrased with the strong imperative verb at the start (**dirue**) followed by the chiastic and asyndetic phrasing of **Maurorum attegias, castella Brigantum**. The rare word **attegias** ('huts': only found here in Latin literature) suggests that the father is up to speed with the jargon.

197 The 'eagle' (**aquilam**) was the legionary standard, which was held by the senior centurion (*primipilus*): this office was usually held for a year and the holder was then given equestrian rank thereafter

(*OCD* s.v. 'primipilus') and a generous gratuity which helps to explain the transferred epithet **locupletem** ('rich') here applied to the eagle itself. To the youth the age of sixty (**sexagesimus annus**) will seem centuries away and having to fight Moors and Brigantes in the meantime might not be an attractive prospect.

198–9 The laborious work of the camp is well brought out by the sequence of long syllables and the assonance of 'o' in **lōngōs cāstrōrum**. The impersonal verb **piget** is well-chosen: related to the adjective *piger* ('sluggish, lazy') it suggests weary distaste.

199–200 The mere sound of the horns and trumpets is enough to loosen the bowels of the nervous soldier. The *cornu* was a form of trumpet, while the *lituus* was a deeper instrument closer to the Alpenhorn. The Pavlovian response of the bowels is well brought out by the epithet **trepidum** applied to the **ventrem** and the vivid term **solvunt**. The father shows a grotesque lack of sensitivity in saying this to his son.

200–1 **pares** is second person singular present subjunctive of *paro* ('you should get') and the subjunctive **possis** has final quality ('something for you to be able to sell'). **pluris** is a genitive of price and is qualified by **dimidio** ('by a half': ablative of measure of difference) so that the phrase comes to mean 'to sell with a 50 per cent profit'.

201–2 Some trades involving pollution and/or foul smells (such as tanning: see **corium** at 204) were forced to operate away from the city across the Tiber. **fastidia** indicates 'distaste' (cf. 14.184) and there was a general feeling in Rome that trade was not appropriate for an aristocrat. The sentence is (literally) construed thus: 'let not distaste (**fastidia**) for any trade (**mercis ullius**) which has to be moved (**ablegandae**: a gerundive of obligation) beyond the Tiber come over you (**te . . . subeant**)'.

203–5   **discriminis** is a partitive genitive with **aliquid**: the sentence is paced to throw the emphasis on the enjambed and contrasted terms **unguenta et corium**. **corium** is the term for a 'skin' or 'hide' and so indicates tanning. The enjambement of **qualibet** (going with **re**) throws emphasis on the word and heightens the sense of 'any at all'.

205–6   We are made to wait for the father's words of wisdom. **semper** is hyperbolic, and the suggestion that Jupiter would say this 'if he were a poet' is a humorous aside. **dis atque ipso Iove** has the effect here of turning a broad comment ('worthy of gods') into a tiny caricature of the greatest of the gods scribbling – with the added insult that that great god would be capable of nothing better than the trite line which follows.

207   *nēmō* is the usual scansion of the word, but elsewhere in Juvenal (e.g. 6.17) it is scanned *nēmŏ*. This line is perhaps taken from another source – as befits this highly unoriginal father.

208–9   These lines may be a later interpolation but the sentence is similar to many other such sentiments by Juvenal concerning the corruption of the young (e.g. 1.78) and putting the cynicism into the mouths of nurses is a nice touch of scathing humour. There is also a nice balance between the boys (**pueris**) being 'shown' this while the 'girls' (**puellae**) 'learn' it.

208   The word **assae** ('dry-nurses') goes with **vetulae**. Note how the chiasmus enacts the crawling boys being enclosed by the nurses.

209   **alpha** and **beta** are the first two letters of the Greek alphabet, here standing for the most rudimentary education in literacy. Roman education and culture were mostly bilingual in Latin and Greek.

210   The juxtaposition of **instantem monitis** stresses the father's insistence. **quemcumque** goes with **parentem** – 'any parent, whoever he is' – suggesting that the poet would be fearless in his rebuke.

A Level

211 **possem** is an imperfect subjunctive in an implied conditional: 'I could say [if I had the chance]'. *vanus* denotes 'void' or 'pointless' but here means 'foolish, silly'. The line is striking for the preponderance of monosyllabic words (**sic ... dic ... quis te**) suggestive of the finger-jabbing tone.

212 **festinare** recalls the earlier (176–7) assertion that people who want to be rich want to get rich quickly (repeated with **properantis** in 178): the son will grow up at his own pace and does not require pressure to advance in avarice ahead of his years. **iubet** is also critical: the father is being 'told' by others what to do.

212–13 The short syllable on the end of *praestŏ* is not uncommon in Juvenal (cf. *malŏ* at 14.153), especially in the fifth foot of the line. The four-word statement across the line-end has great force: **praesto** means 'I guarantee, vouch for' and (with **securus** in 213) suggests 'you need have no fears on that account', while **magistro** is well juxtaposed in enjambement with **discipulum** to enact the truth that the pupil may come after the master but will be his superior (**meliorem**), with *futurum* understood. **abi** can be taken literally ('go away [and leave the lad alone]!') but also has the colloquial sense 'away with you!', 'enough!'.

213–14 The son is superior to his father in avarice as some warrior sons outdid their fathers in the age of the Trojan War: a playful comparison of high and low. **Aiax** (Ajax) was the son of Telamon, ruler of Salamis, while **Achilles** was the child of Peleus and the sea-nymph Thetis. It was foretold that the son of Thetis would be greater than his father – and Peleus is seen as weak and helpless in much of the *Iliad*. In Homer's *Iliad*, Ajax cuts a massively heroic figure and is several times (2.768, 7.289, 13.321, 17.279) named as the greatest fighter among the Greeks after Achilles. The names are listed in chiastic order here, with the sons framing the fathers, and there is neat variation of vocabulary in **praeteriit** and **vicit**.

A
Level

215–16   parcendum est teneris recalls Virgil's advice to farmers (*Georgics* 2.363) on tending young plants. The phrasing here is highly moralistic and rhetorical with a nice metaphor of 'filling the bone-marrow' (**implevere** is third person plural form of the perfect tense of *impleo*, equivalent to *impleverunt*). The two words denoting evil (**mala nequitiae**) are juxtaposed for effect.

216–17 The youth's young adulthood is marked by the clipping of his first beard (*depositio barbae*), which was kept as a memento when the youth assumed the *toga virilis*. Young men are said to have kept trimmed beards until the white hairs of middle age (at about forty) and thereafter gone clean-shaven: see 6.105–6n. Elsewhere (8.165–6) the first beard is regarded as the time to cease from youthful folly (cf. 14.12n.), while here it is seen as the entry to adult misbehaviour.

217   admittere here means 'to allow access'. **longi** (genitive agreeing with **cultri**) is focalized: to the youth the blade would appear long at such close quarters.

218–19 The misbehaviour predicted here consists of lying on oath as a witness (**testis**) for cash (**vendet**) and doing so even though the rewards are small (**summa / exigua**) and the oath is sworn on a major deity (Ceres). The points are enhanced by the enjambement of **exigua** and by the **et** suggesting that he would perjure himself 'even' before Ceres. Ceres was the Roman goddess of agriculture, parallel to the Greek deity Demeter (*OCD* s.v. 'Ceres') and an oath in her name was especially binding. The first 'i' in *periuria* is consonantal and lengthens the first syllable by position so that the word is scanned *pēriūriă*: compare *ābiĕtĕ* (from *ăbiĕs*) at Virgil *Aeneid* 2.16.

219 Touching the altar of a god while swearing an oath made the oath even more binding. Touching the foot of the statue as well made it even stronger, and the polysyndeton **aramque pedemque** shows the perjurer's brazenness.

A
Level

220–4 A husband will murder a wealthy wife for her dowry. A dowry given by the bride's father was returned to him if she died, but a dowry given to her by other people was kept by the widower. If the wife's father had predeceased her then the dowry would be kept by the widower. In cases of divorce a wife would need to recover her dowry both to give to her next husband and to support herself in the meantime – considerations which would not apply in the case of death. Some authors alleged that men married a wealthy woman for her money and these 'dowried wives' then exercised control over their gold-digging husbands as the dowry would have to be returned if the marriage ended (see e.g. 6.136–41).

220–1 **elatam** (from *effero*) simply means 'carried out' but here has the sense of 'carried out for her funeral'. **vestra** suggests that the son is still living with his father. The force of the sentence is increased with the words **iam … si … subit** – she is 'already' dead if she (so much as) enters the threshold accompanied by (**cum**) the fatal dowry. The bride was carried over the threshold to mark a new marriage and the doorposts were decorated lavishly (cf. 6.51–2). **subit** may bear a sinister sense of 'undergo' which joins well with the compound adjective **mortifera** (literally 'death-bringing' from *mors* + *fero*). The lethal force of the dowry is well conveyed by the joining of the ponderous adjective to the dissyllabic **dote** – so much harm from so small a word.

221–2 The husband is imagined strangling his bride, with the girl verbally enveloped by the murderous fingers (**quibus … digitis**) which frame the sentence. The daughter-in-law (*nurus*) of 220 is now simply 'her' (**illa**). *premo* here has the specific sense of 'throttle, strangle': the detail **per somnum** adds vivid detail of the murder as taking place while the victim is asleep.

222–4 Note the contrast between the addressee (the father) who thinks wealth should be acquired by effort and the son (abruptly

A Level

referred to as **illi**) who wants a faster route (**brevior via**) to riches (cf. 14.176-7). The difficulty of obtaining wealth by seeking it abroad is well conveyed by the heavy syllables of the gerundive **acquirenda** (cf. 14.114-16, 14.125) and by the polysyndeton in **terraque marique**. Here, the epic journey and risk is contrasted with a 'shorter route' which skips along in (mostly) light syllables (**brĕvĭor vĭă**).

224 Another sweeping generalization, with *est* to be understood. The contrast (between the honest toil of the father and the quick fix of the criminal son) assumes that theft is easy, using juxtaposition to contrast **nullus** and **magni**. The genitive case of **sceleris** is possessive: crime has many attributes, perhaps, but hard work is not one of them.

224-5 The speaker puts words into the mouth of his interlocutor as at (e.g) 14.153-5, with his denial emphasized by the pair of strong verbs (**mandavi . . . suasi**) framing line 225, as well as the four heavy spondees of **māndāvī dīcēs ōlīm nēc. olim** means here 'one day' in the future: elsewhere in Juvenal it refers to the past (e.g. 6.42, 14.180).

226 A metrically inelegant line, with final monosyllable and clash of ictus and accent in the last two words, suggestive perhaps of the finger-wagging indignation of the speaker. Here, the son's condition is classed as 'a bad mind' (**mentis . . . malae**) – i.e. insanity. **causa . . . et origo** here heightens the emphasis and extends the weight of the accusation being levelled throughout this line at the monosyllabic culprit **te. penes** means 'in the hands of'.

227-32 Another generalization about 'anyone' before rounding once again on the addressee with a second-person verb and pronoun (**revoces . . . te**).

227 The sentiment is given added weight by the heavily spondaic rhythm. *praecipio* here means 'instruct' (cf. *praecepta* at 14.189) and is picked up and varied with **monitu** in 228.

228 There is a sharp change of tense from the perfect **praecepit** to the present tenses **producit . . . dat . . . effundit**, suggesting that the previous instruction leads to the present (unintended and unwelcome) consequences. **laevo** (literally 'left-side') here means 'harmful, pernicious'.

229 This avaricious father has sons who aim to double their **patrimonia**. **dat libertatem** (230) is the main verb governing the infinitive: 'since (**quippe**) he gives them the freedom to double their inheritance by fraud . . .'.

230–1 **curriculo** ('chariot') is dative case with **effundit habenas**: he 'lets the reins go in the case of the chariot'.

231–2 The metaphor of the chariot-race continues, with the appropriate terms **revoces** (to recall the riders after a false start), **subsistere** ('to stop running'), **rapitur** ('is swept along' with a faint echo of the more literal sense of *rapio* ('I seize, steal') which fits the context) and **metis** ('turning-posts': see next note).

232 The line is elegantly constructed around the central strong present indicative verb **rapitur**, with both 'you' and the 'turning-posts' abandoned in different ways. The turning-posts were the crucial and critical elements in the race: if the chariot went too close to one it might crash and wreck all chances of victory, whereas if the chariot passed too widely then it would give another driver the chance to undertake and seize the lead: see *OCD* s.v. 'horse- and chariot-races'. **relictis** here focalizes the exultant speed of the driver who has successfully negotiated the turn and left the posts (safely) behind. **contempto** marks a sour point – the son who perhaps owes everything to his father is now full of contempt for him and has left him in disgust.

233–331: Parents need to beware of teaching their children to grow up rapacious and impatient to inherit the family estate – by murder if

A
Level

necessary. People take huge risks to make money in trade and their antics are more outrageous than anything seen on the stage. If they make a fortune they can never relax for fear of being robbed. How much money does anyone need? Only enough to satisfy hunger, thirst and cold.

Satire 15

This remarkable study of anger and superstition is unusual for being wholly focused on somewhere other than Rome, as well as for the attention given to the value of *humanitas* and the uplifting promotion of human kindness. The targets of the satire are (as elsewhere) folly and vice: the folly of worshipping false gods and the vice which allows us to see other people as a meal. The poet no doubt knew that he could count on his readers sharing his revulsion at what is (by any standards) appalling behaviour: his criticism of the Egyptians begins (1–12) with their (relatively harmless) religious ideas about animals, before moving onto their murderous rage towards humans. His moralism may push us into thinking that in this poem the speaker is a construct of the Roman racist bigot, regaling his listeners with prurient details of what he claims to despise. It is again worth remembering that what matters most is the poetry: and whatever degree of 'sincerity' which lies behind it matters less than the sheer brilliance of the execution.

1–26: The Egyptians are a strange race. They worship animals as if they were gods but have no qualms about eating people. Ulysses' tales of cannibalism must have provoked angry disbelief among his Phaeacian audience but such things really happen in Egypt.

27–32 This is a story from recent times – a tale worse than any tragedy.

27-9 The speaker moves from the distant past to recent (**nuper**) events, from Ulysses' tall and uncorroborated tales to events (from a specific place and time) committed by a whole people.

27 **nos** (plural for singular) is not needed as it is in the verb **referemus** but is put here (in emphatic position) to mark the difference between Ulysses and the poet himself, whose tale is **miranda quidem** but very much true – a contrast which is stressed further with the repetition of **nos** at 29. Lucius Aemilius Iuncus was consul in 127 CE and this passage helps to date the poem, although **nuper** is not specific and 'recently [in comparison to the Trojan War]' allows a lot of latitude. **consule Iunco** is an ablative absolute construction.

28 Coptus is in Upper Egypt on the river Nile: **super** means 'beyond'. The speaker sets the scene: he names the area, specifies that it had city-walls and adds that it was 'boiling hot' (**calidae**). Saying that Egypt is hot may seem a cliché, but *calidus* also means 'passionate, angry' which will be seen to the full in what follows.

29 The *cothurnus* was a loose boot worn by tragic actors: it is here used in metonymy to mean 'tragedy'. The phrase **cunctis . . . cothurnis** (ablative of comparison with **graviora**) has obvious alliterative and assonant force. *vulgus* is often pejorative (see 2.74, 3.36-7, 15.126, Horace *Odes* 3.1.1) and this will be reinforced as the mob-violence becomes lynch-justice and finally cannibalism.

30-1 Tragedies generally focus on the actions of individuals or families, but both Aeschylus' *Persians* and Euripides' *Bacchae* could be seen as exceptions to the generalization. Presumably the poet is thinking of the ghastly violence which is often depicted in tragedy and comparing it favourably with the even ghastlier case he is about to narrate.

30 A *syrma* was a long robe worn by tragic actors, here used (like **cothurnis** in 29) metonymically for 'tragic role'. The verb **volvas** primarily means 'roll' but here has the metaphorical sense of 'read'

A
Level

from the action of unrolling a written scroll (cf. 6.452, 10.126). The resulting phrase is a mixed metaphor ('you scroll through the trailing robes') complete with a mythological *exemplum* which neatly suggests the style as well as the content of tragedy. **Pyrrha** and her husband Deucalion were the only people allowed to survive the great flood sent by the gods and their task was then to form a new human race by throwing stones which turned into people and so **a Pyrrha** stands for 'from the start of the human race'.

31–2 **accipe** is a didactic imperative, while **exemplum** indicates a paradigm or significant case produced by the **dira feritas** of the Egyptians: **nostro . . . aevo** is in contrast to the centuries since Pyrrha.

33–92 *The feud and its murderous consequences, including cannibalism*

33–5 Ombi and Tentyra are termed **finitimos** and (if our identification of them is correct) are about ten miles apart: Tentyra is modern Denderah, north of Coptus, while Ombi is (probably) modern Negadeh. This sentence is remarkable for its sequence of parallel phrases, in which the rising list of **simultas**, **odium** and **vulnus** are all subjects of the singular verb **ardet**, and in which **finitimos** agrees with the place-names **Ombos et Tentyra**.

33 **vetus** and **antiqua** reinforce each other but are not synonymous: see 6.21n.

34 **immortale** and **numquam sanabile** are saying similar things in different terms: the hatred is 'undying' while the 'wound' can 'never be healed'. The terms are sardonic here as the ensuing fight will cause people – if not their hatred – to die and will inflict very literal 'wounds' on each other.

35 **ardet** as a metaphor for the blaze of passion is common – cf. 1.45, 15.52 – but also extends the metaphor of **vulnus** as the 'wound' is now feverish and inflamed.

A Level

35-7 The sparring of the two places is stressed in **utrimque . . . vicinorum . . . uterque**, the strength of feeling is evoked in **furor . . . odit**, and mob madness is enacted in the juxtaposition **furor vulgo. inde** is picked up by **quod** after the caesura (the **furor** is 'from the fact that each place . . .'). **vīcīnōrum** takes up the final two feet of line 36 with a solemn fifth-foot spondee (cf. 14.115). The collective nature of the madness is stressed with the use of the place-names (**Ombos et Tentyra**), the pejorative noun **vulgo** and then the agency ascribed to the **locus** which is said to hate, to believe and to worship (**odit . . . credat . . . colit**) as a person in itself (**ipse**). Understand *est* with **furor**.

36-8 The **numina** at issue were possibly crocodiles: the Ombi worshipped them, while the Tentyrites hated and hunted them.

37-8 *habere* here means 'regard': it is appropriate that the trouble started during a religious festival (**tempore festo**). **sed** has a conversational tone in starting the story after the general remarks ('but anyway . . .').

39-40 Which side started it? The speaker avoids attributing blame at this point, simply describing the two sides as **alterius** and **inimicorum**: lines 73-6 suggest that it was the Tentyrites who first attacked the Ombites (and so **alterius** here means Ombites while **inimicorum** refers to the Tentyrites), but it was clearly important for the poet *not* to apportion blame yet in this tale of mutual hatred and reciprocal brutality. The sentence is construed thus: 'the **occasio** seemed (**visa** (*est*)) worth taking (**rapienda**) by all (**cunctis**) the chiefs and leaders'. 'Seize an opportunity' is natural language in English (and Latin) but the verb *rapere* also has a sense of violence – it was not just the opportunity being 'seized' here – and a sense of urgency. The warring tribes are dignified with the terminology: **populi . . . primoribus ac ducibus** elevates men who will form a riot and forces the reader to see that this was as much a state-action, whose blame lay with the leaders, as the behaviour of a disorderly mob. The syncopated rhythm of the last two feet, with its clash of ictus and accent, is effective in marking the strife.

41 The line splits at the caesura into the two parallel phrases denoting the festivity in general (**laetum . . . diem**) and the culinary delights in particular (**magnae . . . cenae**). The emphasis is on pleasure (**laetum . . . gaudia**) and cheerfulness (**hilarem**) and the final word **cenae** neatly looks forward to the details of the dinner in the following line – and also to the cannibal 'feast' which is to come.

42 **sentirent** is sinister: the Ombites will not even 'be aware of' their lavish party once the enemy strike. The set-up here sounds Roman, with portable tables (**mensis**) loaded with food and diners reclining on a couch (**toro**), but the outdoor location is specified as being at 'temples and crossroads' as described also in Herodotus (2.35.4). Temples are of obvious significance in the political and religious life of the people, but crossroads (**compita**) are also vital places to meet and gossip in ancient times (see 6.412) and even have their own cult (the *Lares Compitales*: see *OCD* s.v. 'Lares').

43 *pervigil* is a strengthened form of *vigil*, meaning 'awake all night long', a sense strengthened by the addition of **nocte ac luce**. **pervigili** agrees with **toro** and is a transferred epithet (it is the diner rather than the couch who stays awake), just as **iacentem** suggests both the reclining person and the couch which is its grammatical referent. **nocte ac luce** is a pleasing phrase with **nocte** looking back towards **pervigili** and **luce** looking forward to the sun which shines in 44.

44 The slow pace of time is evoked in the spondaic rhythm of the second and third foot, while the sudden discovery is enhanced by the dactylic present tense **invĕnĭt**. Note also the pathetic fallacy whereby the sun 'sees' what goes on.

44–6 quantum has the sense of 'to the extent that' and qualifies the generalization ('so far as I have observed [but I may have not seen enough to judge]'). **famoso** ('disreputable') suggests that he relies on the word of others for his judgement. The poet's language is highly critical with each key term first in its clause: Egypt is **horrida** (understand *est*), and the people possess great **luxuria** – and neither is a laudable characteristic. **horrida** suggests aversion to personal luxury and grooming as at 6.10. **sane** ('to be sure') concedes that Egyptians are rustic in this way and the rest of the parenthesis is devoted to the **luxuria**, with the 'golden' line 46 packing quite a punch in the promotion of **barbara**, the effective final juxtaposition of **turba Canopo** and the understated **non cedit**. A contrast is here set up between the native Egyptians (the **barbara . . . turba**) and the Greek inhabitants of Canopus, a disreputable (**famoso**) resort twelve miles from Alexandria.

47–8 The didactic imperative phrase **adde quod** (cf. 14.114) introduces another factor into the situation: lines 40–2 explained the objective, while lines 47–8 explain the timing with the focalized term **facilis** reporting the attackers' view of the situation. The drunkenness of the Ombites is brought out in the tricolon crescendo of (a) **madidis**, (b) **blaesis**, (c) **mero titubantibus**. *madidus* (literally 'soaked') is common in the sense 'drunk' (cf. 6.297): *blaesus* properly denotes 'mispronouncing one's words' and was commonly used for drunken word-slurring. *titubare* (literally 'to totter, stagger') is another obvious symptom of intoxication and is to be expected if they are drinking unmixed wine (**mero**). Notice how the awkward rhythm of the ending of 47 mirrors the unsteadiness of the drunken people.

48–51 The moods of the two sides are contrasted with **inde . . . hinc . . .**: merriment on the one hand (**inde**) and 'ravenous hatred' on the other (**hinc**).

A
Level

48–9 Dancing was not something which decent Roman men went in for (cf. *OCD* s.v. 'dancing') but the point is not laboured as the Egyptian character has already been damned.

49–50 The dancing is well described with imagery which is visual (**nigro . . . flores . . . coronae**), auditory (**tibicine**), and even olfactory (**unguenta . . . flores**). **qualiacumque** is depreciatory in tone and here suggests that the Egyptians were not fussy about the quality of their perfumes. **multaeque in fronte coronae**, if taken literally, adds a touch of absurdity with its image of plural garlands on one brow, although the point of **multae** is presumably to stress that this party was a lavish affair, despite the unflattering description of the fragrances (**qualiacumque**). The occasion is not specified: **tempore festo** (38) suggests a religious festival.

51 After the joyous pleasure comes the painful hatred. *ieiunus* literally means 'hungry', and the literal sense is to the fore here both because the Tentyrites are not sharing the feast and also because their enemies the Ombites will eat their flesh.

51–2 The battle begins with taunts (**iurgia**): the start of the battle is marked both by **prima** and also by the enjambed **incipiunt**. Ancient military battles often began with the trumpet-call and so the term **tuba** here indicates 'beginning'. **ardentibus** (cf. 35n.) varies the metaphor of **ieiunum**, while the specific **odium** is now widened to more general **animis** which has the sense of 'anger' and 'passion' (cf. 6.285) as well as simply 'heart' or 'mind'. *rixa* (found also at 61 below) is more commonly found in contexts of private quarrels (especially involving drink) rather than in military action and reminds us that this is an impromptu brawl.

53 The word-order mirrors the action as the shouting (**clamore**) spreads to the other side (**pari**) and then leads to action (**concurritur**). **concurritur** is an impersonal passive: cf. 6.269, 304–5, AG §208d. **vice** + genitive means 'as a substitute for'.

54–6 The narrative passes immediately from the attack to the outcome and the casualty rate is shown in two ways: **paucae sine vulnere malae** and **vix cuiquam aut nulli . . . integer**.

55–6 **vix cuiquam aut nulli** (literally 'hardly anyone or nobody') is colloquial for 'hardly anyone'. The poet neatly juxtaposes **nulli toto** for effect and leaves the nose dangling at the end of the line before completing the phrase with the enjambed **integer**: for a split-second it seems that the fighters have lost the nose altogether: the same effect is repeated in **vultus / dimidios** in 56–7.

56–8 Facial disfigurement is further described to the reader, who is addressed with the indefinite second-person subjunctive **aspiceres** – the imperfect subjunctive making the verb vividly present in sense ('[if you were here] you would be seeing ...'). The phrase **cuncta per agmina** picks up and varies **toto certamine** by adding that the injuries were sustained by all ranks. The injuries are horrific: faces torn in two (**dimidios**), unrecognizable features (**alias facies**), bones showing through broken cheeks. **alias** (literally 'changed') is something of an understatement before the grisly detail to follow: **genis** could mean either 'cheeks' or 'eyes', but the detail of 'gaping bones' supports the former more than the latter, although the hint of 'eyes' is picked up in **oculorum**. J. juxtaposes **ossa genis** for vividness: **ruptis . . . genis** is an ablative absolute ('once the cheeks had been smashed'). The final image of this sentence is one of fists full of blood from eye-sockets, thus saving the worst until last. **hiantia** and **plenos** also suggests eating – *hio* is used of gaping mouths desperate for food (10.231) and *plenus* is often used of the satisfied diner, which looks forward to the feast to come.

59–60 The fighters inflict grotesque injuries, and yet (**tamen**) the matter is not serious enough as nobody has died: **ludere . . . pueriles** frames lines 59 to sum up ironically the gruesome contents of lines

51–8, while **pueriles ... acies** would suggest boys playing soldiers. **ipsi** is important, showing that the sentence is focalized through the eyes of the combatants themselves – which also explains the subjunctive **calcent** as reporting their own thoughts, conveyed with the brutal alliterative phrase **cadavera calcent**. The verb *calco* (derived from *calx* ('heel')) denotes both superiority and contempt.

61–2 **sane** is ironic, appearing to make the outrageous statement reasonable (seen also in the quasi-philosophical **ergo** in 62), with oxymoron of 'sensibly' against the **rixantis ... turbae. quo** here means 'for what purpose?' (see 14.135). **rixantis** picks up *rixae* (52) while **turbae** picks up *turba* (45): **tot milia** is hyperbolic but they make up one singular **turbae**. The short concluding phrase **si vivunt omnes** is devastatingly simple.

62 The thirst for death makes the fighting fiercer. **ergo** is sardonic, while the final monosyllables (**et iam**) show the narrative picking up speed.

63 The poet makes it clear here and in 64–5 (**domestica ... tela**) that the battle is not planned as the fighters have to search for rocks from the ground. **inclinatis ... lacertis** is a vivid touch – the arms are bent back to give greater force to the throw – and the hyperbaton lengthens the phrase as the thrower stretches his arms.

63–4 *torqueo* is often used of throwing spears (which are spun by the thrower) but the word also means 'to torture' which adds force here.

64–5 Line 64 has no strong caesura (there is a weak caesura in the third foot but none in the fourth) and the final five-syllable word is ungainly (cf. 6.71, 6.373, 15.4). *domestica seditio* means 'civil strife' (as opposed to external warfare): here the adjective **domestica** is going with **tela** and has the sense of 'usual, familiar' as well as 'locally sourced' (cf. 14.32).

A Level

65–7 The plural **saxa** (63) are now downgraded to a single stone (**lapidem**). We have to understand a verb for 'they threw' with **quales** ('not the sort of rocks which Turnus and Ajax threw …'). Rock-throwing was a standard part of epic combat, often coming between spear-throwing and close combat, and the greater the warrior, the bigger the stone. **Tydides** ('son of Tydeus') is a patronymic name referring to Diomedes, and this epic material adds to the mock-epic tone of the passage. The size and weight of the rock are evoked with the heavy preponderance of spondees in 66, and the moment of impact is conveyed in the alliterative and assonant **percussit pondere coxam**. The word **coxam** (hip) is not a poetic term and ends line 66 with jarring bathos.

65–8 Epic commonly depicts heroes of the past as greatly superior to modern humans (see introductory note to 6 and cf. 6.9n.). The satirist makes good use of the trope here, mocking the puny moderns in contrast to their epic forebears, using epic terms to describe what the heroes did and more modest language (**sed quem valeant emittere**) of the Egyptians. Line 68 spells out the degeneration and ends with a wonderful touch of satire in the final word **natae**: this word agrees with **dextrae** which is feminine in gender but there is a clear implication that these moderns are women rather than (real) men, a taunt found also in Homer (*Iliad* 2.235, 7.96).

69 The speaker now undercuts his recent promotion of 'ancient (good) vs contemporary (bad)', by telling us that things were already (**iam**) going downhill even when Homer was alive, thus mocking the very trope he has been using.

70 The language here recalls the 'golden age' theory which was explored and sent up at 6.1–24. The idealization of the past is as old as Homer: see for instance Nestor's nostalgic reminiscences at Homer *Iliad* 1.260–73. The assumption here is that physical toughness is accompanied by moral strength and that *luxuria* softens muscles as much as morals. *pusillus* is a striking term: it is probably the diminutive of *pullus* which is itself a word for what is small (such as a foal or chick) or else a euphemistic term for a small person. Taking this word with **homines** produces something of a satiric oxymoron, but it also bears out the view that early man was bigger and stronger (cf. 6.9 where early women produced 'large babies').

71 The gods respond to both forms of human weakness: they 'laugh' at them for being puny and 'hate' them for being wicked, in chiastic order (**malos ... pusillos ... ridet ... odit**) and with chuckling assonance of *-et et*. The singular **deus** – qualified by **quicumque aspexit** – suggests that divine attention towards us is not great. This neatly sums up the attitude of the satirist himself who (like a divine viewer) regards folly and vice with laughter and loathing.

72 The speaker now picks up his narrative from line 65 with a deft apology for the interruption: the ironic conversational style suggests that he is speaking extempore. *deverticulum* is a metaphor for a digression in writing or a diversion from work: both senses are in play here. **fabula** is used often of a tale with a point to it – as in Horace *Satires* 1.1.70, 1.1.95, 2.6.78 (*fabellas*).

73-4 After the impromptu rock-throwing, the fighting now uses 'proper' weapons (**ferrum ... sagittis**) to repel the attack. **subsidiis aucti** is a vivid detail and also explains the sudden increase in courage shown in **audet**, while **promere ferrum** is a military phrase for what is becoming less of a scuffle and more of a battle. **pars altera** is non-specific (see 39–40n.) but line 75 makes it clear that it refers to the Ombites. **infestis** may seem redundant – arrows are usually 'hostile' – but here the word reinforces both **audet** and **pugnam** which frame it, showing that it took courage (**audet**) to face the fight (**pugnam**). **instaurare** is a good word to use: properly it means 'to resume' or 'repeat' and here it shows that the arrival of the reinforcements (**subsidiis aucti**) is making them 'renew' their efforts.

75 The Ombites are referred to by the name of their town, as at 35 and also with Egypt itself (45). **instantibus** is good military vocabulary while **praestant** is more elevated vocabulary than simply *dant*. The effect throughout this passage is of a pompous narrator overdoing his efforts, with booming assonance such as **prae<u>stant</u> in<u>stant</u>ibus**.

76 The poet takes a whole line to name the Tentyrites (who are the subject of **praestant** in 75), reminding us (cf. 33) that they were neighbours (**vicina**). Tentyra is described in almost idyllic terms, with shady palms as protection against the heat (cf. 28n.). There may also be a sly dig at the expense of the Tentyrites: *palma* was (6.323) a sign of victory but here they are facing defeat. **umbrosae . . . palmae** is to be read as a genitive of quality ('Tentyra of the shady palm') rather than dative with **vicina** ('close to the shady palm': see AG §345): **palmae** here is a collective singular.

77–8 The narrative is forceful with strong present tense verb-forms at the start of the lines and effective enjambement of **cursum /** **praecipitans**. The hapless victim is anonymous (**quidam**) and his mishap is blamed on his excess of fear – a point which both focalizes the tale and also increases our empathy. **praecipitans** is transitive here with **cursum** ('hurrying his course'). Falling in running-races is not uncommon – but this fall is fatal and the framing of the sentence with the parallel verbs (**labitur . . . capiturque**) marks the sealing of his doom.

78–81 The cannibal feast is described in grisly detail. First the hacking of the man from being a singular **illum** into the plural **frusta** **et particulas** – where **frusta** denotes large chunks and the diminutive **particulas** shows these in turn subdivided into bite-sized morsels, with the word order mirroring the action. The narrator then speculates on the reason for this, with the same contrast of singular and plural in **multis ... unus**. The quick eating of the man is conveyed in a single dissyllabic word **edit**: but the poet also gives the detail of the bones being gnawed (note the rare word **corrosis**, the assonant **corrosis ossibus** with its onomatopoeic sibilance as they chew) as they eat him all up (**totum**), bones and all. The subject of this long sentence is the singular **turba**, acting with one will and in victory (**victrix**).

81–3 The cannibalism was worse than it might have been as the man was not even cooked before being eaten, owing to their impatient refusal to wait for the cooking process. The two ways of cooking meat are listed in mock-serious discussion: boiling (**decoxit**) or roasting (the verb has to be assumed from the culinary term **veribus** ('roasting spits')). The poet then stretches out the phrase **longum usque adeo tardumque ... / expectare** to enact the lengthy wait envisaged: **longum** simply means 'lasting a long time' (as at 6.292) while **tardum** focalizes their impatience, suggesting 'slow'. The final phrase (**contenta cadavere crudo**) has crunching onomatopoeia and ends the sentence with mounting horror: they are (a) contented, (b) with a corpse and (c) it is not even cooked.

84 The tone becomes sarcastic – they treat people badly but at least they respected fire, which had its divine representative in the figure of Vulcan (see *OCD* s.v. 'fire'). *violo* is a religious term ('pollute').

85–6 The Titan Prometheus stole fire from the gods and gave it as a gift (**donasti**) to mankind: for this he was chained to a pillar, his liver was eaten daily by an eagle and regenerated every night (Hesiod *Theogony* 506–616). There is added detail here: instead of simply stealing fire from heaven, Prometheus stole it **summa caeli ... de parte**, emphasizing the effort which Prometheus put into the theft. The balancing pair **caeli** and **terris** is neatly placed at the same

A Level

metrical position in the two lines, immediately before the caesura in the third foot. **donasti** is the shortened form of *donavisti* (from *dono*).

85 The apostrophe to Prometheus is an epic device (see 6.7-8n.) and suggests an (ironic) attachment of the poet towards the Titan, as developed in the next line.

86–7 **elemento** refers to one of the four elements (earth, air, water and fire) which made up all matter. There is something comic about using the interpersonal term **gratulor** for a physical element; and the use of the first-person verbs is also an ironic touch of mock-emotion, complete with the ludicrous image of the philanthropic Prometheus 'rejoicing' that this cannibalism involved no fire.

87–8 **mordere cadaver** adds the detail of 'biting' (as well as consuming) the body: and the overcoming of natural distaste is conveyed in **sustinuit** which is emphasized in enjambement. Line 88 is framed by two strong verbs and the line is making the surprising statement that these people, not only *could* do this, but found it delightful, with the corpse (**cadaver**) now turned into meat (**carne**).

89–92 The final vignette of this section develops the thought of line 88: far from being a minority taste, these men were even queuing up to taste the drops of blood which were all that remained.

89 The deed was described as a *scelus* twice in 29–30. In the phrase **quaeras et dubites** the second person subject here is no longer Prometheus but the reader (as at 14.143, 14.149–50).

90 The 'pleasure' (**voluptatem**) is contained inside the **prima ... gula** in verse as in life, and the spondaic rhythm suggests the savouring of the meal. For the choice of **gula** here as the organ of greedy eating cf. 14.10.

90–1 **ante** points to the temporal sequence whereby the man, who was standing at the back of the queue 'just before', finds the body 'by now' (**iam**) all eaten up and only gets a taste (**gustat**) at the very end of this long sentence and his long wait.

91–2 The dead body is now termed **corpore** in opposition to the **sanguine** (placed in identical position on the next line) which is all that is now left. **ductis** here indicates tracing a line in the earth. The choice and use of words is effective as the disappointed cannibal, expecting flesh, only had blood; he also only gets 'some' (**aliquid**) blood; and only a taste of it (**gustat**) rather than a drink, after putting his fingers through the earth (with **terram digitis** juxtaposed to enact the movement).

93–174: The speaker goes on to describe the cannibalism of the Vascones, which was forced upon them by starvation and so was excusable (unlike that of the Egyptians). He ends the poem more positively: humans must show compassion towards each other, or they behave worse than wild animals.

Vocabulary

An asterisk * denotes a word in OCR's Defined Vocabulary List for AS, although the meanings given in this book are not necessarily the same as the ones in the DVL as this vocabulary is tailored to this text. This vocabulary lists every word in the text. Nouns are listed with their genitive singular, and verbs are listed with all their four principal parts. Adjectives are listed with the endings of the different genders (e.g.: bonus -a -um) except where the three genders are the same in the nominative where the genitive is listed (e.g.: iners, inertis). This vocabulary also lists the places where words occur so that students may quickly compare and contrast the poet's use of each word in different contexts. Long vowels are marked as such with macra (e.g. mōs).

*a *prep.+abl.*	from, by
*abeō, abīre, abiī, abitum	depart, go away (14.149)
*abī! (imperative of abeō)	go away! (14.213)
ablēgō, ablēgāre, ablēgāvī, ablēgātum	move, relocate (14.202)
abstineō, abstinēre, abstinuī, abstentum	abstain from (14.99)
*absum, abessē, āfuī	be missing (6.294)
absūmō, absūmere, absumpsi, absumptum	consume, use up (15.91)
*ac	and
*accipiō, accipere, accēpī, acceptum	receive (6.113), take (6.76, 14.191), hear (15.31)
Accius -ī *m.*	Accius (6.70)
accusō, accusāre, accusāvī, accusātum	make an accusation (6.243)
acer, acris, acre	nasty (6.109), fierce (15.62)
acerbus -a -um	harsh (14.18)
acervus -ī *m.*	heap, pile (6.364)

Achilles -is *m.*	Achilles (14.214)
aciēs, aciēī *f.*	battle-formation (15.60)
acquirō, acquirere, acquisīvī, acquisītum	acquire, gain possessions (14.115, 125, 223)
***ad** prep.+acc.*	to, towards
adde quod (imperative from **addō**)	consider also the fact that (14.144, 15.47)
***adeō**	to such an extent (6.50, 59, 15.82)
***adhūc**	still, to this day (15.35)
admittō, admittere, admīsī, admissum	allow access (14.217)
admoveō, admovēre, admōvī, admōtum	bring in, recruit (14.12)
adnotō, adnotāre, adnotāvī, adnotātum	take notice of (14.195)
adōrō, adōrāre, adōrāvī, adōrātum	worship (6.47, 14.97)
adulter, adulterī *m.*	adulterer (6.404)
adultera -ae *f.*	adulterous woman (14.25)
aedēs, aedis *f.*	temple (14.90)
aedificātor -ōris *m.*	builder (14.86)
Aegyptus -ī *f.*	Egypt (15.45)
Aelia -ae *f.*	Aelia (6.72)
Aemilius -a -um	Aemilian (bridge: 6.32)
Aenēās -ae *m.*	Aeneas (15.67)
aenum -ī *n.*	bronze pot (15.81)
***aequus -a -um**	fair, just (14.15)
āēr, āeris *m.*	air, sky (6.99)
aestivus -a -um	of the summer (14.131)
aetas, aetātis *f.*	age, generation (6.23), passing of time (14.161)
aevum -ī *n.*	time, era (15.32)
***afferō, afferre, attulī, allatum**	bring (14.78, 198)
afficiō, afficere, affēcī, affectum	excite (14.24)
affirmō, affirmāre, affirmāvī, affirmātum	claim (6.58)
affōr, affāri, affātus sum *deponent*	address, speak to (14.211)
age *imperative*	see **causam ago**
agellus -ī *m.*	small plot of land (6.57)
***ager, agrī** *m.*	rural location (6.56), field (14.151), land (14.159,172)
agitō, agitāre, agitāvī, agitātum	plot, intend (6.251)
***agmen, agminis** *n.*	battle-line (15.56)

*agō, agere, ēgī, actum	do (6.58, 6.403), carry out (14.149)
Aiax, Aiacis m.	Ajax (14.213, 15.65)
āla -ae f.	upper arm, shoulder (14.195)
ālea -ae f.	gambling with dice (14.4)
aliēnus -a -um	belonging to somebody else (6.21)
aliquando adverb	sometimes (6.360)
*aliquis, aliqua, aliquid	some (6.15, 280), somebody, something (14.21, 134, 15.92), anyone, anything (14.203)
aliter adverb	differently (6.11)
*alius, alia, aliud	other (6.23, 67), different, altered (15.57)
alpha	alpha (first letter of Greek alphabet: 14.209)
*alter, altera, alterum	another person (6.17), a second (14.131, 141, 170), the other of two (15.73)
alternus -a -um	alternating, reciprocal (6.268)
*altus -a -um	high (6.31, 14.88, 185)
Ambrosius -ii m.	Ambrosius (6.77)
*ambulō, ambulāre, ambulāvī, ambulātum	move, walk (6.305)
āmens, āmentis	crazy (14.94)
*amīca -ae f.	female friend (6.353)
*amō, amāre, amāvī, amātum	love (6.62, 75, 112, 253, 404)
*amōr, amōris m.	love (6.275), desire (14.139, 227)
amplexus -ūs m.	sexual embrace (6.65)
amplus -a -um	substantial (14.171)
*an	or (6.61, 75, 14.18)
*angustus -a -um	narrow (6.78), scanty (6.357)
anhēlō, anhēlāre, anhēlāvī, anhēlātum	pant, gasp (6.37)
anima -ae f.	soul (14.16)
animal, animālis n.	animal (14.76)
*animus -ī m.	spirit (6.97, 285, 14.15, 15.52), mind (14.33, 119)
*annus -ī m.	year (14.10, 197)
*ante preposition	before (14.209)
*ante adverb	earlier (15.90)
antīcus -a -um	ancient (6.21)
Antiphatēs -ae m.	Antiphates (14.20)
antīquus -a -um	ancient (6.45, 15.33)
apertus -a -um	open, unguarded (6.18)

*apud *prep.+acc.*	among (6.91, 15.31)
Āpula -ae *f.*	Apula (6.64)
*aquila -ae *f.*	eagle (14.197)
*āra -ae *f.*	altar (14.219)
aratrum -ī *n.*	plough (14.181)
*arbor, arboris *f.*	tree (14.80)
arbustum -ī *n.*	vineyard, plantation (14.144)
arca -ae *f.*	money-chest (6.363)
arcānus -a -um	mystical (14.102)
ardeō, ardēre, arsi	burn, blaze (14.24, 118, 15.81), be passionate (15.35, 52)
argenteus -a -um	made of silver (6.24)
*argentum -ī *n.*	silver (6.355)
arista -ae *f.*	ear of corn (14.147, 183)
*arma, armōrum *n.pl.*	armour (6.264, 292), implements (14.5)
Armenius -a -um	Armenian (6.407)
arō, arāre, arāvī, arātum	plough (14.160)
artifex, artificis *m.*	craftsman (14.116)
arvum -ī *n*	field (6.410)
arx, arcis *f.*	headland, citadel (14.87)
aspiciō, aspicere, aspexī, aspectum	see (6.261, 15.56), look on (15.71)
assa -ae *f.*	dry-nurse (14.208)
assiduus -a -um	unceasing, incessant (6.248, 14.118)
ast	but (6.67, 15.78)
Astraea -ae *f.*	Astraea (goddess of justice: 6.19)
Asylus -ī *m.*	Asylus (6.267)
*at	but (14.189)
Ātellānus -a -um	in Atellan farces (6.71)
āthlēta -ae *m.*	athlete (6.356)
atque	and
attegia -ae *f.*	hut (14.196)
attendō, attenderē, attendī, attentum	pay attention (6.66)
attingō, attingere, attigī, attactum	touch, have contact with (14.106)
attollō, attollere	raise up, build (14.95)
attrītus -a -um	worn down (6.108)
auctiō -ōnis *f.*	auction (6.255)
auctor -ōris *m.*	authority (14.33)
auctus -a -um	reinforced (15.73)
*audax, audācis	bold, daring (6.284, 399)

*audeō, audēre, ausus sum	dare (6.97, 15.74)
*audiō, audīre, audīvī, audītum	hear (14.200)
aulaeum -ī *n.*	theatre-curtain (6.67)
aurātus -a -um	gilded (6.48)
*aut	or
*aut ... aut	either ... or (6.272)
*autem	in fact (14.83), moreover (14.100)
Autonoē -ēs *f.*	Autonoe (6.72)
autumnus -ī *m.*	autumn (14.190)
*auxilium -ī *n.*	help (14.183)
avāritia -ae *f.*	avarice, miserliness (14.108)
avārus -a -um	avaricious, greedy (14.111, 119, 178, 228)
avis -is *f.*	bird (14.82)
balteus -ī *m.*	sword-belt (6.256)
barba -ae *f.*	beard (14.216)
barbarus -a -um	barbarian (15.46)
barbātus -a -um	bearded (6.16, 14.12)
Bathyllus - ī *m.*	Bathyllus (6.63)
beātus -a -um	happy, well-off (14.120)
bēta *indeclinable*	beta (second letter of the Greek alphabet: 14.209)
*bibō, bibere, bibī	drink (6.304)
bīnī -ae -a	two (14.163)
blaesus -a -um	slurring words (15.48)
bōlētus -ī *m.*	mushroom (14.8)
bombȳcinus -a -um	silken (6.260)
*bonus -a -um	good (14.204)
bōs, bovis *m./f.*	cow, bull (14.146)
*brevis -e	short (6.289, 14.223)
Brigantes -um *m.pl.*	Brigantes (British tribe: 14.196)
būcina -ae *f.*	trumpet (14.152)
bullātus -a -um	wearing a child's locket (14.5)
buxus -ī *f.*	comb (14.194)
cadāver, cadāveris *n.*	corpse (14.78, 15.60, 83, 87)
caecus -a -um	blind (6.265)
caedō, caedere, cecīdī, caesum	slaughter (6.48)
*caelum -ī *n.*	sky (6.11, 283, 14.97, 15.85)

caeruleus -ea -eum	blue (14.128)
Caetrōnius -ī *m*.	Caetronius (14.86, 92)
Caiēta -ae *f*.	Caieta (14.87)
calcō, calcāre, calcāvī, calcātum	trample underfoot (15.60)
calidus -a -um	hot (15.28)
cālīgō, cālīgāre	be dizzy (6.31)
camīnus -ī *m*.	forge (14.118)
cāneō, cānēre, cānuī	be white (14.144)
*canis -is *m*.	dog (14.77)
Canōpus -ī *m*.	Canopus (6.84, 15.46)
cantō, cantāre, cantāvī, cantātum	sing (6.74), be musical (6.398)
cānus -a -um	old, aged (14.10)
*capiō, capere, cēpī, captum	capture (15.78), captivate (6.103)
capistrum -ī *n*.	harness (6.43)
Capitōlium -ī *n*.	Capitoline Hill with its temples (14.91)
caprea -ae *f*.	deer (14.81)
captātor -ōris *m*.	legacy-hunter (6.40)
*caput, capitis *n*.	head (6.17, 301, 14.194), person (6.49)
carcer, carceris *m*.	slaves' quarters (14.24)
careō, carēre, caruī, caritum	go without (14.39), escape suffering from (14.156)
carō, carnis *f*.	meat, flesh (14.98, 15.88)
casa -ae *f*.	cottage (14.167)
castellum -ī *n*.	fort (14.196)
castigō, castigāre, castigāvī, castigātum	chastise, punish (14.126)
*castra -ōrum *n.pl*.	army-camp (14.198)
castus -a -um	chaste, pure (6.287)
casula -ae *f*.	small cottage (14.179)
catēna -ae *f*.	chain (14.23)
cathēdra -ae *f*.	chair (6.91)
caulis -is *m*.	cabbage (6.18)
*causa -ae *f*.	court-case (6.241, 14.192), cause (14.173, 226)
causam agō, agere, ēgī, actum	plead a court case (14.192)
in causā esse	be responsible (14.105)
cavō, cavāre, cavāvī, cavātum	hollow out (6.248)
*cēdō, cēdere, cessī, cessum	concede (6.57), be inferior to (15.46)
*celer, celeris, celere	swift (15.75)
Celsus -ī *m*.	Celsus (6.245)

*cēna -ae f.	dinner (14.130), meal (14.170, 15.41)
cēnō, cēnāre, cēnāvī, cēnātum	dine (14.13)
census -ūs m.	wealth (6.362, 14.176, 227)
cēra -ae f.	wax (writing tablets: 14.29, 14.191)
Cerēs, Cereris f.	Ceres (goddess of agriculture: 6.50, 14.219)
cērōma, cērōmatis n.	clay wrestling floor (6.246)
*certāmen, certāminis n.	fight, struggle (15.55)
*certē adverb	certainly (6.28)
*certus -a -um	firm, sure (14.113)
cervīcal -ālis n.	pillow, cushion (6.353)
cessō, cessāre, cessāvī, cessātum	rest, be inactive (6.67)
*cēterī, cēterae, cētera	the others (14.107)
chīronomos -os -on	in pantomime style (6.63)
choraulēs -ae m.	piper (6.77)
Chrȳsogonus -ī m.	Chrysogonus (6.74)
*cibus -ī m.	food (14.79)
cicōnia -ae f.	stork (14.74)
cinaedus -ī m.	catamite, pervert (14.30)
cista -ae f.	chest (6.44)
citharoedus -ī m.	lyre-player (6.76)
cito adverb	quickly (14.27, 31, 177)
*clāmō, clāmāre, clāmāvī, clāmātum	shout (6.283)
*clāmor -ōris m.	shout (15.53)
clāmōsus -a -um	yelling, shouting (14.191)
claudō, claudere, clausī, clausum	enclose (6.4, 68)
*coepī, coepisse defective	begin (6.106, 113, 14.217)
coetus -ūs m.	gathering (6.399)
*cōgitō, cōgitāre, cōgitāvī, cōgitātum	think of, intend (6.39)
*cōgō, cōgere, coēgī, coactum	compel (14.124, 135)
Collinus -a -um	on the Quirinal Hill in Rome (6.291)
collis -is m.	hill (6.296, 14.179)
collum -ī n.	neck (14.146)
*colō, colere, coluī, cultum	worship (14.103, 15.38), inhabit (15.76)
color -ōris m.	positive spin (6.280)
colubra -ae f.	snake (6.29)
*comes, comitis m./f.	companion (6.20, 353)
comētēs -ae m.	comet (6.407)

comitōr, comitārī, comitātus sum	accompany (6.82)
commūnis -e	shared, held in common (6.4)
cōmoedus -ī *m.*	comic actor (6.73)
*comparō, comparāre, comparāvī, comparātum	compare, find equal (14.20)
compitum -ī *n.*	crossroads (15.42)
complexus -ūs *m.*	embrace (6.279)
compōnō, compōnere, composuī, compositum	compose (6.244)
compositus -a -um	composed of (6.13)
concēdō, concēdere, concessī, concessum	allow (14.7)
concha -ae *f.*	shell (6.304)
conchis -is *f.*	bean (14.131)
concumbō, concumbere, concubuī, concubitum	sleep with (6.406)
concurrō, concurrere, concurrī, concursum	charge at (15.53)
concutiō, concutere, concussī, concussum	shake vigorously (6.22)
condiō, condīre, condīvī, condītum	marinade (14.8)
condūcō, condūcere, condūxī, conductum	hire (6.352–3)
conduplicō, conduplicāre, conduplicāvī, conduplicātum	double (14.229)
*conferō, conferre, contulī, collatum	bring (14.223)
confundō, confundere, confūdī, confūsum	jumble up, confuse (6.284)
*coniunx, coniugis *m./f.*	husband (6.85, 98), wife (6.255)
cōnōpēum -ī *n.*	infant's cradle (6.80)
conscendō, conscendere, conscendī, conscensum	embark (on a ship: 6.98)
conscius -a -um	aware of (6.271), acting as accomplice (14.28)
constans, constantis	unflinching, firm (6.93)
constō, constāre, constitī	cost (6.365), consist of (14.17)
*consul, consulis *m.*	consul (15.27)
*consumō, consumere, consumpsī, consumptum	consume, eat (14.128)
contemnō, contemnere, contempsī, contemptum	disrespect (6.22, 14.100), disregard (6.90), despise (14.232)

contentus -a -um	satisfied (6.54, 14.179, 15.83)
contexō, contexere, contexuī, contextum	join together (14.27)
contingō, contingere, contigī, contactum	be granted (6.49, 14.184), touch (6.50), stain (6.288)
conveniō, convenīre, convēnī, conventum	agree (6.281)
conventum -i *n.*	meeting (6.25)
convomō, convomere, convomuī, convomitum	vomit on (6.101)
Coptus -ī *f.*	Coptus (15.28)
corium -ī	hide (14.204)
cornu -ūs *n.*	horn (14.199)
corōna -ae *f.*	garland (6.51, 15.50)
corōnātus -a -um	garlanded (6.297)
*corpus, corporis *n.*	body (14.16, 15.91)
corrōdō, corrōdere, corrōsī, corrōsum	chew up (15.80)
corrumpō, corrumpere, corrūpī, corruptum	corrupt (14.32)
corymbus -ī *m.*	cluster of berries (6.52)
cothurnus -ī *m.*	buskin, actor's shoe (15.29)
coxa -ae *f.*	hip (15.66)
*crēdō, crēdere, crēdidī, creditum	believe (6.1, 275, 14.119, 149, 203, 15.37, 59), regard (14.220)
crescō, crescere, crēvī, crētum	grow (14.116–7, 139)
*crīmen, crīminis *n.*	crime (6.23, 285, 294)
crista -ae *f.*	crest (6.256)
crūdus -a -um	raw, uncooked (15.83)
crūs, crūris *n.*	leg (6.256)
crux, crucis *f.*	cross (14.77)
cubīle, cubīlis *n.*	bed, couch (14.82)
culīna -ae *f.*	cuisine, food (14.14)
culmen, culminis *n.*	roof (14.89)
culmus -ī *m.*	straw (6.6)
culter, cultrī *m.*	knife (14.217)
cultus -a -um	tilled, arable (14.159)
*cum *conjunction*	when (6.2, 5, 17, 31–2, 264, 271, 303–4, 14.10, 33, 80, 83, 136, 138, 141, 216), since (14.110, 15.37)
*cum *prep.+abl.*	with (6.400, 14.131, 200, 221)

cūnae -ārum *f.pl.*	cradle (6.89)
*cunctī -ae -a	all (6.410, 15.29, 39, 56)
cuneus -ī *m.*	wedge-shaped group of seats in theatre (6.61)
cupīdō, cupīdinis *f.*	desire (14.175)
*cupiō, cupere, cupīvī, cupītum	desire (14.13)
*cūra -ae *f.*	anxiety (14.157)
*cūrō, cūrāre, cūrāvī, cūrātum	care (6.300)
curriculum -ī *n.*	chariot (14.231)
cursus -ūs *m.*	rapid speaking (14.27), running, course (15.77)
curtus -a -um	incomplete (14.166)
curvō, curvāre, curvāvī, curvātum	bend (6.262)
curvus -a -um	curved (14.86)
cyclas, cycladis *f.*	female outer garment (6.259)
Cynthia -ae *f.*	Cynthia (6.7)
damnō, damnāre, damnāvī, damnātum	condemn (6.84)
damnōsus -a -um	ruinous (14.4)
*dē *prep.+abl.*	from (6.33, 76), made of (6.45)
dēbilitās -ātis *f.*	weakness, infirmity (14.156)
deciēns	ten times (14.28)
dēcoquō, dēcoquere, dēcoxī, dēcoctum	boil (15.81)
dēcrescō, dēcrescere, dēcrēvī, dēcrētum	decline, diminish (15.69)
decus, decoris *n.*	honour, distinction (6.255)
dēdūcō, dēdūcere, dēduxī, dēductum	lead (14.104)
dēformis -e	ugly (6.107)
dēgenerō, dēgenerāre, dēgenerāvī, dēgenerātum	decline (14.14)
*dein	then (15.53)
*deinde	afterwards (6.19)
dēliciae -ārum *f.pl.*	affectation, preciosity (6.47), delicate skin (6.260)
dens, dentis *m.*	tooth (14.11)
densus -a -um	thick (6.52, 263, 14.144)
dēprendō, dēprendere, dēprendī, dēprensum	catch (somebody doing wrong: 6.285)
*deus -ī *m.*	god (14.206, 15.38, 71)
dēverticulum -ī *n.*	digression (15.72)

dēvius -a -um	remote, off the beaten track (14.75)
*dextra -ae *f.*	right hand (15.67)
*dīc (plural dīcite) *(imperative)*	tell me! (6.29, 265, 281–2)
*dīcō, dīcere, dīxī, dictum	call (6.104), say (6.405, 14.150, 180, 225), name (14.26)
dictō, dictāre, dictāvī, dictātum	dictate (6.245, 14.29)
*diēs -ēī *m.*	day (15.41)
differō, differre, distulī, dīlātum	postpone (14.130)
digitus -ī *m.*	finger (6.27, 14.222, 15.92)
dignus -a -um	worthy, deserving (6.50, 61, 14.1, 206), suitable (6.249)
dīligō, dīligere, dīlexī, dīlectum	love (6.72)
dīluvium -ī *n.*	flood (6.411)
dimidium -i *n.*	a half (14.201)
dīmidius -a -um	half-sized (6.257, 14.132), cut in half (15.57)
dīripiō, dīripere, dīripuī, dīreptum	compete for (6.404)
dīruō, dīruere, dīruī, dīrutum	demolish (14.196)
*dīrus -a -um	dreadful, appalling (15.32)
discipulus -ī *m.*	pupil, student (14.213)
*discō, discere, didicī	learn (6.66, 14.9, 209)
discrīmen, discrīminis *n.*	distinction, difference (6.301, 14.203)
*dissimilis -e	dissimilar, unlike (15.68)
distō, distāre	be different (14.98)
*diū *adverb*	for a long time (6.2)
dīversus -a -um	different (6.257)
*dīves, dīvitis	rich (14.176)
*dīvitiae -ārum *f.pl.*	wealth (6.300, 14.135)
*dō, dare, dedī, datum	give (6.27, 354, 359, 14.30, 158, 163, 230)
*doceō, docēre, docuī, doctum	teach (14.18, 125)
domesticus -a -um	domestic, of the home (14.32), familiar (15.64)
domī *locative*	at home (6.357)
*domina -ae *f.*	mistress (6.30)
*dominus -ī *m.*	master (6.4, 14.145, 169)
*domus -ūs *f.*	home (6.3, 85, 14.148)
dōnō, dōnāre, dōnāvī, dōnātum	give (6.356, 15.86)
*dormiō, dormīre, dormīvī, dormītum	sleep (6.34, 89, 269)
dōs, dōtis *f*	dowry (14.221)
*dubitō, dubitāre, dubitāvī, dubitātum	doubt, wonder (15.89)

*dubius -a -um	uncertain (14.111, 136)
*dūcō, dūcere, duxī, ductum	marry (6.28), lead (14.188), drag (15.91)
dulcis -e	pleasing, sweet (6.38)
*dum	since (14.92, 95)
duo, duae, duo	two (6.20)
*dūrus -a -um	hard (6.98, 102, 290)
*dux, ducis *m.*	general (6.400, 15.40)
*ē *prep.+abl.*	out of (6.364)
ēbrius -a -um	drunk (6.300)
Echīōn -onis *m.*	Echion (6.76)
ēdiscō, ēdiscere, ēdidicī	learn fully (14.101, 124)
edō, esse, ēdī, ēsum	eat (15.80, 88)
ēducō, ēducāre, ēducāvi, ēducātum	produce (15.70)
efferō, efferre, extulī, ēlātum	carry out for burial (14.220)
*effugiō, effugere, effūgī	escape from (14.157)
effundō, ēffundere, effūdī, effūsum	slacken (reins: 14.230)
egens, egentis	poor, needy (14.137)
*ego *pronoun*	I (6.282–3, 14.154, 224)
ēgregius -a -um	outstanding (14.115)
elementum -ī *n.*	atom (14.17), rudiment (14.123), element (15.86)
ēmittō, ēmittere, ēmīsī, ēmissum	hurl (15.67)
endromis, endromidis *f.*	track-suit (6.246)
*enim	for (6.300, 14.109, 127, 224)
*eō, īre, īvī, itum	go (6.409, 14.122)
Eppia -ae *f.*	Eppia (6.82, 104)
*eques, equitis *m.*	knight (6.279)
ergastulum -ī *n.*	dungeon (14.24)
*ergo	therefore (14.79, 92, 119, 140, 15.62, 71)
*errō, errāre, errāvī, errātum	wander (6.101)
error -ōris *m.*	fault (14.15)
ēsuriens -entis	hungry (14.127)
*et	and, also
*etiam	even (14.161)
eurus -ī *m.*	the east wind (14.186)
Euryalus -ī *m.*	Euryalus (6.81)
*ex *prep.+abl.*	from out of (14.204)

Vocabulary   145

ex quō	ever since (6.294)
exagitō, exagitāre, exagitāvī, exagitātum	agitate, drive mad (6.29)
exardescō, exardescere, exarsī, exarsum	blaze with passion (6.103)
excerpō, excerpere, excerpsī, excerptum	pick out (6.62)
***excipiō, excipere, excēpī, exceptum**	pick up (6.409)
***excitō, excitāre, excitāvī, excitātum**	awaken (14.191)
***exemplum -ī** n.	example (14.32), instance, case (14.120, 15.32)
exerceō, exercēre, exercuī, exercitum	practise (14.108, 15.60)
exhauriō, exhaurīre, exhausī, exhaustum	drain (6.363)
exigō, exigere, exēgī, exactum	demand (6.35)
exiguus -a -um	tiny (14.155, 219)
exitus -ūs m.	way out (6.33)
exodium -ī n.	comic play (6.71)
expavescō, expavescere, expāvī	fear (6.361)
***expectō, expectāre, expectāvī, expectātum**	expect (6.75, 14.25), wait for (6.274, 15.83)
exprimō, exprimere, expressī, expressum	create an image of (6.81)
exsorbeō, exsorbēre, exsorpsī	drink up (6.277)
exstinguō, exstinguere, exstinxī, exstinctum	kill (6.8)
exstō, exstāre, exstitī	exist (6.15)
exsurgō, exsurgere, exsurrexī	get up (6.305)
extorqueō, extorquēre, extorsī, extortum	force, extort, torture (6.54)
exultō, exultāre, exultāvī	rejoice (15.87)
faber, fabrī m.	blacksmith (14.116)
Fabius -ī m.	Fabius (6.266)
fābula -ae f.	tale, narrative (15.72)
faciēs -iēī f.	face (6.107, 401, 15.57)
***facilis -e**	easy (15.47)
***facinus, facinoris** n.	act (6.294)
***faciō, facere, fēcī, factum**	do (6.282), make (6.110, 405, 14.80, 151), invent (6.409), commit (a crime: 14.185, 15.31)

factum -ī *n.*	deed (6.271)
falx, falcis *f.*	scythe (14.149)
Falernus -a -um	Falernian (6.303)
***fallō, fallere, fefellī, falsum**	trick, deceive (14.109)
falsus -a -um	false, lying (14.218)
***fāma -ae** *f.*	repute (6.55), rumour (6.408), reputation (6.90, 14.1), gossip (14.152)
famēlicus -a -um	starved, hungry (14.146)
famēs -is *f.*	hunger (6.360, 14.84)
fāmōsus -a -um	notorious (6.83, 15.46)
famula -ae *f.*	servant (14.81)
far, farris *n.*	grain, plain food (14.155)
fascia -ae *f.*	bandage (6.263)
fastīdium -ī *n.*	distaste (14.184, 201)
fātum -ī *n.*	destiny (14.137, 158)
***fēlix, fēlīcis**	fortunate, happy (6.258, 14.21, 119)
***fēmina -ae** *f.*	woman (6.60, 242, 362)
fēmineus -a -um	female (6.246)
fenestra -ae *f.*	window (6.31)
fera -ae *f.*	wild beast (6.6)
***ferē** *adverb*	virtually (6.242), usually, as a rule (14.173)
feritās -ātis *f.*	savagery, brutality (15.32)
***ferō, ferre, tulī, lātum**	carry (6.9, 14.30), endure (6.30, 14.198), attend (6.399)
ferreus -a -um	iron (6.23)
***ferrum -ī** *n.*	steel (blades: 6.112, 14.174, 15.73), iron (14.22)
***festinō, festināre, festināvī, festinātum**	hurry (14.84, 212)
festus -a -um	festival (15.38)
fētus -a -um	pregnant (14.167)
fētus -ūs *m.*	offspring (14.78)
fibula -ae *f.*	pin (6.73)
fīcēdula -ae *f.*	fig-pecker (bird: 14.9)
Fīdēnae -ārum *f.pl.*	Fidenae (6.57)
***fidēs -ēī** *f.*	loyalty (14.166)
figō, figere, fixī, fixum	set up (6.78), implant (14.2)
***filia -ae** *f.*	daughter (14.26)
***filius -ī** *m.*	son (14.94)

fīlum -ī n.	slice, filament (14.133)
fingō, fingere, finxī, fictum	invent, make up (6.272)
*fīnis -is m.	end (14.190) (in plural: territory (14.142))
fīnitimus -a -um	neighbouring (15.33)
*fīō, fierī, factus sum	become (6.77, 254, 14.117, 176-7), take place (6.255), happen (6.41, 402)
flagellum -ī n.	lash, whip (14.19)
flāvus -a -um	blonde (6.354)
flētus -ūs m.	weeping (6.276)
Flōrālis -e	belonging to the Floralia (6.250)
flōs, flōris m.	flower (15.50)
fluctus -ūs m.	wave (6.92)
fluō, fluere, fluxī, fluxum	flow (6.295)
focus -ī m.	fireplace (15.83)
foedus -a -um	disgraceful (14.152)
fons, fontis m.	source (6.286), spring (14.104)
forma -ae f.	appearance (6.103)
formīca -ae f	ant (6.361)
formīdō, fōrmīdinis f.	fear, panic (15.77)
formō, formāre, formāvī, formātum	construct (6.244)
forsan adverb	perhaps (6.14)
*fortasse adverb	perhaps (6.27)
*fortis -e	brave (6.97)
*fortūna -ae f.	position in life (6.287), wealth (14.113)
Fortūna -ae f.	Fortune (goddess: 14.90)
*forum -ī n.	court (6.68)
*frangō, frangere, frēgī, fractum	break up, shatter (14.93, 161), weaken (6.299)
*frāter, frātris m.	brother (14.169)
fraus, fraudis f.	deceit (14.229)
fremitus -ūs m.	roar (6.261)
frīgidus -a -um	cold (6.2)
*frīgus, frīgoris n.	cold (6.360)
fritillus -ī m.	dice-box (14.5)
frons, frondis f.	foliage (6.6)
frons, frontis f.	brow, forehead (15.50)
frūgī indeclinable	thrifty (14.111)
frustum -ī n.	piece of food (14.128, 15.79)
*fuga -ae f.	retreat (15.75)

*fugiō, fugere, fūgī	flee (6.20), run away from (6.253)
fulcrum -ī *n*.	bed-head (6.22)
fūmō, fūmāre, fūmāvī	smoke (14.171)
fūr, fūris *m*.	thief (6.17)
*furor, furōris *m*.	madness (14.136, 15.36)
Fuscīnus -ī *m*.	Fuscinus (14.1)
Gabiī -ōrum *m.pl.*	Gabii (6.56)
galea -ae *f.*	helmet (6.108, 262)
galeātus -a -um	wearing a helmet (6.252)
banniō, gannīre	yelp like a dog (6.64)
*gaudeō, gaudēre, gāvīsus sum	take pleasure in (6.75, 102, 14.18), be happy (15.84)
*gaudium -ī *n*.	pleasure (6.365, 15.41)
gelō, gelāre, gelāvī, gelātum	freeze (6.95)
geminus -a -um	double (6.305)
gemitus -ūs *m*.	groaning, moaning (6.271)
gemō, gemere, gemuī, gemitum	grunt (6.267)
gena -ae *f.*	cheek, eye (15.58)
generōsus -a -um	noble (14.81)
genius -ī *m*.	protecting spirit (6.22)
*genus, generis *n*.	race (15.69)
*gerō, gerere, gessī, gestum	do, carry out (15.2)
gestus -ūs *m*.	motion, gesture (6.72)
gibbus -ī *m*.	lump (6.109)
glaciēs -iēī *f.*	ice (14.186)
gladiātor -ōris *m*.	gladiator (6.110)
*gladius -ī *m*.	sword (14.162)
glans, glandis *f.*	acorn (6.10)
Glaphyrus -ī *m*.	Glaphyrus (6.77)
glēbula -ae *f.*	small clod of earth (14.166)
Graecus -a -um	Greek (6.16, 14.89)
grandis -e	plentiful (6.79), massive (6.302, 14.171), broad (14.195)
grassor, grassārī, grassātus sum	prowl (14.174)
grātulor, grātulārī, grātulātus sum	congratulate (15.86)
grātus -a -um	welcome, pleasing (14.183)
*gravis -e	disgusting (6.99), overbearing (6.270), horrifying (15.29)

gula -ae f.	throat (14.10, 15.90)
Gurges, Gurgitis m.	Gurges (name of Fabius at 6.266)
gustō, gustāre, gustāvī, gustātum	taste (14.85, 15.92)
guttur, gutturis n.	throat, neck (6.105)
habēna -ae f.	rein (14.230)
*habeō, habēre, habuī, habitum	have (6.13, 358), contain (6.61, 268), possess (14.140, 207), consider (15.37)
*habitō, habitārē, habitāvī, habitātum	be housed (14.92)
habitus -ūs m.	clothing, outfit (6.267, 14.110)
haereō, haerēre, haesī, haesum	cling to, stick (14.2), be stuck for an idea (6.281)
Hannibal -alis m.	Hannibal (6.291)
harēna -ae f.	arena (6.251)
*haud (+adjective)	not (6.7, 14.136)
Herculēs -is m.	Hercules (14.90)
hērēs, hērēdis m.	heir (6.39, 14.4)
Hernicus -a -um	from the Hernici tribe (14.180)
Hesperides -um f.pl.	Hesperides (14.114)
hesternus -a -um	from yesterday (14.129)
Hibērīna -ae f.	Hiberina (6.53)
*hīc adverb	here, in this situation (6.280, 15.84)
*hic, haec, hoc	this
hilaris -e	cheerful, joyous (15.41)
*hinc	from here (6.295-6, 14.13, 82), on this side (15.51)
hiō, hiāre, hiāvī	gape open (15.57)
Hispulla -ae f.	Hispulla (6.74)
Homērus -ī m.	Homer (15.69)
*homō, hominis m.	human being (6.12, 284, 14.184, 15.70), man (6.47, 14.112)
honestus -a -um	respectable (6.95)
horridus -a -um	shaggy, hairy (6.10), unkempt (15.44)
*hortor, hortārī, hortātus sum	urge (14.121)
*hortus -ī m.	garden, smallholding (6.18, 14.172)
hūmānus -a -um	human (14.98, 175)
humilis -e	modest, humble (6.287)
*humus -ī f.	ground (15.63)
Hyacinthus -ī m.	Hyacinth (6.110)

*iaceō, iacēre, iacuī, iacitum	lie down (6.36, 269, 279, 14.167, 15.43)
iactūra -ae *f.*	loss (6.91)
*iam	by now (6.26, 105, 14.80, 15.56, 91), now (6.43, 304, 15.62), already (6.302, 14.220, 15.69)
iānua -ae *f.*	door (6.79)
ictus -ūs *m.*	blow (6.261)
*idem, eadem, idem	the same (6.112, 402, 14.8, 30, 76, 103, 113, 122)
iēiūnus -a -um	ravenous (15.51)
*igitur	therefore (6.92)
ignāvus -a -um	lazy (14.106)
*ignis -is *m.*	fire (6.3, 15.84)
ignōtus -a -um	unknown, unfamiliar (14.187)
*ille, illa, illud	that (6.22, 53, 85, 250, 269, 358, 14.84, 121, 189, 205, 15.68), he/she/they (6.45, 100, 110–11, 270, 274, 284, 408, 14.76, 123, 221, 223, 15.78)
*illīc	in that place (6.36, 410)
imbuō, imbuere, imbuī, imbūtum	baptize, initiate (14.124)
imitor, imitārī, imitātus sum	imitate (14.107)
immānis -e	brutal, massive (14.162)
immemor, immemoris	having no thought for (6.85)
imminuō, imminuere, imminuī, imminūtum	diminish (14.92)
immodicus -a -um	excessive (14.176)
immortalis -e	undying (15.34)
*imperō, imperāre, imperāvī, imperātum *(+dative)*	control (6.64)
*impetus -ūs *m.*	attack (15.62)
impleō, implēre, implēvī, implētum	carry out (6.249), fill (14.30, 215)
improbus -a -um	wicked (6.86)
*in *prep.+abl.*	in/on
*in *prep.+acc.*	into (6.410, 14.149, 15.78), to (14.130)
*incipiō, incipere, incēpī, inceptum	begin (15.52, 64)
inclīnō, inclīnare, inclīnavī, inclīnātum	bend (15.63)
inclūdō, inclūdere, inclūsī, inclūsum	lock up (14.133)
incumbō, incumbere, incubuī	befall, beset (6.293), devote energy to (14.122)
incūs, incūdis *f.*	anvil (14.118)

*inde	from there (6.62, 14.148, 173, 15.36), then, in turn (14.83)
inde...hinc	on one side ... on the other (14.12–13, 15.48-51)
indulgeō, indulgēre, indulsī, indultum	show regard for (6.86), indulge (6.283)
infans, infantis m./f.	infant (6.9, 81, 14.168)
*inferō, inferre, intulī, illātum	bring in (6.299)
infestus -a -um	hostile, attacking (15.74)
*ingens, ingentis	huge (6.108)
ingrātus -a -um	ungrateful (14.165)
inguen, inguinis n.	groin, crotch (6.301)
*inimīcus -a -um	enemy (15.40)
*inīquus -a -um	serving short measures (14.126)
*iniūria -ae f.	wrongdoing (14.151)
*inquit	he/she said (6.281, 14.153)
insatiābilis -e	insatiable (14.125)
inscriptum -ī n.	branded mark (14.24)
insistō, insistere, institī	stand (6.96)
instaurō, instaurāre, instaurāvī, instaurātum	renew (15.74)
instō, instāre, institī	threaten (6.407), insist on (14.210), press in attack (15.75)
intactus -a -um	untouched (14.194)
integer, integra, integrum	whole, undamaged (15.56)
*inter prep.+acc.	among (6.101), between (14.203, 15.33)
interdum	sometimes (15.44)
*interea	meanwhile (14.138)
*inveniō, invenīre, invēnī, inventum	find (14.75, 15.44)
invertō, invertere, invertī, inversum	turn inside out (14.187)
*invitō, invitāre, invitāvī, invitātum	invite (14.134)
*invītus -a -um	unwilling (14.108)
Īonius -a -um	Ionian (sea: 6.93)
*ipse, ipsa, ipsum	himself, herself, itself, themselves
*īra -ae f.	anger (6.285)
iste, ista, istud	that, those (6.295, 14.179)
iuba -ae f.	beard, barbel (of a fish: 6.40)
*iubeō, iubēre, iussī, iussum	order, direct (6.37, 98, 275, 14.31, 108, 212)
Iūdaicus -a -um	Jewish (14.101)
iūgerum -ī n.	a unit of land (14.163)

Iūlius -a -um	Julian (law: 6.38)
iūmentum -ī *n.*	a beast of burden (14.77, 147)
Iuncus -ī *m.*	Iuncus (15.27)
*iungō, iungere, iunxī, iunctum	join (in marriage: 6.41)
Iūnō, Iūnōnis *f.*	Juno (goddess: 6.48)
Iuppiter, Iovis *m.*	Jupiter (6.15, 59, 14.81, 206)
iurgium -ī *n.*	insult (6.268), taunt (15.51)
iurō, iurāre, iurāvī, iurātum	swear an oath (6.16)
iūs, iūris *n.*	jus, sauce (14.8), law (14.101)
*iustus -a -um	morally correct (6.94)
iuvenca -ae *f.*	heifer (6.48)
*iuvenis -is *m.*	young man, youth (14.7, 23, 107, 121, 191)
iuventa -ae *f.*	youthfulness (6.103)
*iuvō, iuvāre, iūvī, iūtum	please (14.4)
labellum -ī *n.*	lip (6.276)
*lābor, lābī, lapsus sum	slip, fall (15.77)
*labor, labōris *m.*	hard work, toil (6.289, 14.164, 198, 224)
lacerta -ae *f.*	lizard (14.75), mackerel (14.131)
lacertus -ī *m.*	upper arm (6.106, 15.63)
lacessō, lacessere, lacessīvī, lacessītum	assail (6.248)
lacrima -ae *f.*	tear (6.273)
Laelius -ī *m.*	Laelius (14.195)
*laetus -a -um	joyful, happy (14.23, 15.41)
laevus -a -um	harmful (14.228)
Lagus -ī *m.*	Lagus (6.83)
lapis, lapidis *m.*	rock (15.65)
lar, laris *m.*	household god (6.3, 14.20)
Larga -ae *f.*	Larga (14.25)
lassus -a -um	weary, exhausted (14.146)
*lātē *adverb*	far and wide (6.92)
Latīnus -a -um	Latin (6.287)
Latīnus -ī *m.*	Latinus (an actor: 6.44)
*latus, lateris *n.*	groin, flank (6.37)
*laudō, laudāre, laudāvī, laudātum	praise (14.111, 154, 182)
laurus -ī *f.*	laurel (6.79)
lautus -a -um	lavish, expensive (14.13)
lectus -ī *m.*	bed (6.21, 268)

Lēda -ae *f.* — Leda (6.63)

*legō, legere, lēgī, lectum — read (6.277)

Lentulus -ī *m.* — Lentulus (6.80)

Lepidus -ī *m.* — Lepidus (6.265)

lepus, leporis *m.* — hare (14.81)

lēvis -e — smooth-skinned (6.356)

levō, levāre, levāvī, levātum — raise up (14.83)

*lex, lēgis *f.* — law (6.38, 14.100, 177, 193)

libellus -ī *m.* — legal brief (6.244), written request (14.193)

libenter *adverb* — with pleasure, gladly (15.88)

liber, librī *m.* — tree-bark (6.263)

*libertās -ātis *f.* — freedom, license (14.230)

libet, libēre, libuit *impersonal vb.* — it is pleasing (14.142, 15.84)

libīdō, libīdinis *f.* — lust (6.294)

*licet *(+subjunctive)* — although (6.283, 14.12)

līmen, līminis *n.* — threshold (6.47, 52, 14.220)

lintēum -ī *n.* — napkin (14.22)

līs, lītis *f.* — court-case (6.242, 268)

lītigō, lītigāre, lītigāvī, lītigātum — quarrel, argue (6.35)

*lītus, lītoris *n.* — shoreline (14.87)

lituus -ī *m.* — bass trumpet (14.200)

locuplēs, locuplētis — rich, wealthy (14.137, 197)

*locus -ī *m.* — arguing points (6.245), place (15.37)

*longē *adverb* — far off (6.69, 14.89)

*longus -a -um — long (6.65, 78, 292, 14.158, 198, 217, 15.82)

*loquor, loquī, locūtus sum — speak (6.401, 14.115)

lucerna -ae *f.* — lamp (6.305)

lucrum -ī *n.* — profit (14.204)

luctus -ūs *m.* — grief, anguish (14.157)

lūdia -ae *f.* — slave-girl attached to a gladiatorial school (6.104, 266)

lūdō, lūdere, lūsī, lūsum — play (14.4, 168, 15.59)

lūdus -ī *m.* — school of gladiators (6.82), public games (6.87, 352)

lupīnum -ī *n.* — lupin (14.153)

lutum -ī *n.* — mud (6.13)

lux, lūcis *f.* — daylight (14.105, 15.43)

luxuria -ae *f.*	self-indulgence, extravagance (6.293, 15.45)
luxus -ūs *m.*	soft living (6.299)
macellum -ī *n.*	market (6.40)
macer, macra, macrum	thin (14.146)
macula -ae *f.*	stain, blemish (14.2)
madidus -a -um	soaked, drunk (6.297, 15.47)
magis *adverb*	more (6.87, 14.113)
***magister, magistrī** *m.*	expert (6.26), tutor (14.12), teacher (14.212)
magistra -ae *f.*	teacher (6.361)
***magnus -a -um**	big, large (6.9, 39, 410, 14.227, 15.41), great (6.55, 73, 88, 14.32, 224), impressive (14.14), full-grown (14.79, 169)
***māior, māius**	bigger, greater (14.117, 142)
māiōres, māiōrum *m.pl.*	ancestors (14.193)
māla -ae	jaw (15.54)
***mālō, mālle, māluī**	prefer (14.153)
malum -ī *n.*	misfortune (6.109, 292), damage (14.216)
***malus -a -um**	bad (14.226), poor-quality (15.70)
mamilla -ae *f.*	breast (6.401)
mandātum -ī *n.*	instruction (6.354)
***mandō, mandāre, mandāvī, mandātum**	instruct (14.225)
manicae -ārum *f.pl.*	arm-rings (6.256)
manifestus -a -um	obvious (14.136)
Mānīlia -ae *f.*	Manilia (6.243)
mānō, mānāre, mānāvī	flow (6.275)
***manus -ūs** *f.*	hand (6.290, 15.54)
***mare, maris** *n.*	sea (6.94, 283, 14.222)
marītālis -e	marital (6.43)
***marītus -ī** *m.*	husband (6.10, 100, 291, 400)
marmor, marmoris *n.*	marble (14.90, 95)
Mars, Martis *m.*	Mars (6.59)
Marsus -a -um	Marsian (14.180)
***māter, mātris** *f.*	mother (14.28)
māteria -ae *f.*	substance (14.17)

māternus -a -um	of her mother (14.26)
mātrōna -ae *f.*	wife (6.49), married woman (6.250)
mātūrus -a -um	full-grown (14.83), adult (14.216)
Maurī -ōrum *m.pl.*	Moors (14.196)
medicus -ī *m.*	doctor (6.46)
*medius -a -um	in the middle of (6.108, 302, 14.129, 190)
medulla -ae *f.*	bone-marrow, innermost parts (14.215)
Megalēsia, -ium *n.pl.*	Megalesia (6.69)
*melior, melius	better (6.34, 14.6, 95, 143, 158, 212)
*mens, mentis *f.*	mind (14.175, 226)
mensa -ae *f.*	table (6.305, 14.182, 15.42)
*mensis -is *m.*	month (6.406)
mensura -ae *f.*	measurement (14.93)
mercēs, mercēdis *f.*	payment, reward (14.164)
mercor, mercārī, mercātus sum	buy (14.143)
mergō, mergere, mersī, mersum	drown (14.9)
meritum -ī *n.*	service, just desert (14.165)
merum -ī *n.*	undiluted wine (6.303, 15.48)
merx, mercis *f.*	goods, commodity (14.201)
mēta -ae *f.*	turning-post (14.232)
Metellus -ī *m.*	Metellus (6.265)
mētior, mētīrī, mensus sum	measure (6.358)
metuō, metuere, metuī, metūtum	show respect for (14.96, 101)
*metus -ūs *m.*	fear (14.178)
Mīlētos -ī *f.*	Miletus (6.296)
mille (plural milia)	thousand (14.12, 15.61)
minimum *adverb*	hardly at all (6.269)
*minimus -a -um	of no importance (6.91), a tiny amount of (14.124)
*minor, minus	less (14.140, 165)
minōres -um *m.pl.*	descendants (14.189)
minūtal -ālis *n.*	mince (14.129)
*mīror, mīrarī, mīratus sum	admire (14.120, 195), find amazing (15.27)
mīrus -a -um	astonishing (14.24)
misceō, miscēre, miscuī, mixtum	mix (14.174)
miserābilis -e	pathetic (6.65)
mītis -e	gentle (14.15)
*mittō, mittere, mīsī, missum	send (14.147)

modicus -a -um	minor, moderate (14.15)
modius -i *m.*	measuring jar, rations (14.126)
***modo** adverb*	just now (14.86)
***modus -ī** m.*	manner (6.275, 14.117), method, position (6.406), limit, extent (6.359, 14.172)
moecha -ae *f.*	adulterous woman (6.278)
moechus -ī *m.*	adulterer (6.24, 42), lover (6.100, 14.26, 30)
***moenia -ium** n.pl.*	walls (6.83, 15.28)
mollis -e	effeminate (6.63, 300), soft (6.91)
Molossus -a -um	Molossian (14.162)
monita -ōrum *n.pl.*	advice, warnings (14.210)
monitus -ūs *m.*	advice (14.228)
***mons, montis** m.*	mountain (6.58, 14.88, 144)
***monstrō, monstrāre, monstrāvī, monstrātum**	show, point out (6.60, 14.103), demonstrate (6.261, 14.3, 10), teach (14.208)
monstrum -ī *n.*	monster (6.286)
montānus -a -um	of the mountain (6.5)
***morbus -ī** m.*	disease (14.156)
mordeō, mordēre, momordī, morsum	gnaw at (6.302, 15.87)
***morior, morī, mortuus sum**	die (14.137)
***moror, morārī, morātus sum**	linger, delay (6.1)
mortiferus -a -um	lethal (14.221)
mortuus -a -um	dead (15.79)
***mōs, mōris** m.*	way of living (6.84, 298), disposition (6.45, 14.15)
***moveō, movēre, mōvī, mōtum**	arouse (6.71), stir up (6.243), provoke (6.257), shake (14.5)
***mox**	in due course (6.23, 14.99, 125), later on (14.161)
Moysēs -is *m.*	Moses (14.102)
mūcidus -a -um	snotty, mouldy (14.128)
mucrō -ōnis *m.*	blade (14.217)
***mulier, mulieris** f.*	woman (6.252)
mullus -ī *m.*	mullet (6.40)
***multus -a -um**	many
***mūnus, mūneris** n.*	gift (14.183)
mūnusculum -ī *n.*	little gift (6.36)

murmillō -ōnis *m.*	heavy-armed gladiator (6.81)
*mūtō, mūtāre, mūtāvī, mūtātum	change (6.94)
*nam	for (6.105, 254, 14.176, 222, 227, 15.30, 69, 89)
nāris -is *f.*	nose (6.108, 14.194)
*narrō, narrāre, narrāvī, narrātum	tell (6.412)
*nascor, nascī, nātus sum	be born (6.12, 15.68)
nāsus -ī *m.*	nose (15.55)
natō, natāre, natāvī, natātum	swim (14.8)
*nātūra -ae *f.*	nature (14.31)
nātus -ī *m.*	son (6.86)
*nauta -ae *m.*	sailor (6.101)
*nāvis -is *f.*	ship (6.98)
*nē (+subjunctive)	so that ... not (15.40–41, 89)
nebulō -ōnis *m.*	scoundrel, rogue (14.9)
*nec	nor
nec nōn	and furthermore (6.282, 14.130)
nectō, nectere, nexī, nexum	weave (6.51)
nefās *indeclinable*	sin, wickedness (14.188)
*negō, negāre, negāvī, negātum	refuse (14.134)
*nēmō, nēminis	nobody (6.17, 14.207)
neptis -is *f.*	female descendant (6.265)
*neque	and ... not (14.127)
nēquitia -ae *f.*	wickedness (14.216)
*nesciō, nescīre, nescīvī, nescītum	not know (6.247, 301), be unable (14.231)
neu	and so that ... not (14.203)
nīdus -ī *m.*	nest (14.80)
niger, nigra, nigrum	black (15.49)
*nihil *indeclinable*	nothing (6.284)
*nīl	nothing (6.58, 14.97, 185, 15.88), not at all (6.86)
Nīlus -ī *m.*	Nile (6.83)
nimius -a -um	swollen (6.46), excessive (15.77)
Niphātēs -is *m.*	Niphates (6.409)
*nisi	unless (6.250, 14.103)
nitidus -a -um	brilliant, gleaming (6.8, 14.2)
*nōbilis -e	nobly-born (6.81)

*noceō, nocēre, nocuī, nocitum	harm (14.153)
*noctū *adverb*	at night (6.35)
*nōlō, nōlle, nōluī	be unwilling (6.254)
*nōn	not
*nōndum	not yet (6.15–16, 14.11, 215)
*nōnne	surely? (6.34)
*nōs, nōstrī	we, us (14.187, 15.1, 3)
noscō, noscere, nōvī, nōtum	find out, know (6.402)
*noster, nostra, nostrum	our (6.25, 254, 14.16, 91, 172, 15.31, 68)
notō, notāre, notāvī, notātum	observe, mark (15.45)
*nōtus -a -um	well-known (6.42)
novāle -is *n.*	field (14.148)
noverca -ae *f.*	stepmother (6.403)
*novus -a -um	new (6.11, 14.95), last remaining (6.356)
*nox, noctis *f.*	night (6.302, 14.146, 190, 15.43)
nūbēs -is *f.*	cloud (14.97)
nūbō, nubere, nupsī, nuptum *(+dative)*	marry (6.82)
nūdus -a -um	bare, unarmed (15.54)
*nullus -a -um	not any, none (6.13, 33, 36, 242, 294, 357, 14.19, 120, 224, 15.31, 60), nobody (14.165, 15.55)
nūmen, nūminis *n.*	divinity (14.97, 182, 15.36)
numerō, numerāre, numerāvī, numerātum	count (14.133)
*numerus -ī *m.*	rhythmic exercise (6.249)
nummus -ī *m.*	cash, coin (6.364, 14.139)
*numquam	never (14.26, 224, 15.34)
*nunc	now (6.292, 14.29, 172, 189, 15.70)
*nunc … nunc …	now … and then … (14.87–8)
nūper *adverb*	lately, recently (15.27)
nupta -ae *f.*	wife (6.269)
nurus -ūs *f.*	daughter-in-law (14.220)
nūtō, nūtāre, nūtāvī, nūtātum	totter (6.411)
nūtriō, nūtrīre, nūtrīvī, nūtrītum	feed (14.75)
nūtrix, nūtricis *f.*	nurse (6.354)
ō	O! (*vocative exclamation*: 6.46, 14.211)
obscēnus -a -um	filthy (6.298)
obvius -a -um	in one's path (6.412)

*occāsiō -ōnis f.	opportunity (15.39)
occultus -a -um	secret (6.271)
ocellus -ī m.	little eye (6.8, 109)
ōcius comp.adverb	more readily, sooner (6.53)
ocrea -ae f.	greave (6.258)
*oculus -ī m.	eye (6.54, 15.58)
*ōdī, ōdisse	hate (6.272, 15.37, 71)
*odium -ī n.	hatred (15.34, 51)
odor -ōris m.	smell (14.204)
Ogulnia -ae f.	Ogulnia (6.352)
*ōlim	formerly (6.42, 281, 14.180), long ago (6.90), one day in the future (14.225)
olīva -ae f.	olive (14.144)
olla -ae f.	pot (14.171)
Ombi -ōrum m.pl.	Ombi (15.35, 75)
*omnis -e	all, every (6.23, 249, 14.11, 127, 209, 15.30, 62)
opēs, opum f.pl.	wealth (6.88, 14.93, 120)
*oportet, oportēre, oportuit impersonal vb.	it is right (14.207)
*ops, opis f.	help (14.183)
optō, optāre, optāvī, optātum	wish for (14.140)
orbis -is m.	world (6.11, 293, 402)
orbus -a -um	bereaved of her cubs (6.270)
orīgō, orīginis f.	source (14.226)
*ornō, ornāre, ornāvī, ornātum	decorate (6.79)
*ōs, ōris n.	head (6.43), mouth (14.138, 205)
os, ossis n.	bone (15.58, 80)
osculum -ī n.	kiss (6.51)
ostreum -ī n.	oyster (6.302)
ōvum -ī n.	egg (14.85)
pactum -ī n.	agreement (6.25)
paelex, paelicis f.	mistress, lover (6.272)
pāgus -ī m.	country district (14.154)
palma -ae f.	palm (15.76)
palūdātus -a -um	uniformed (6.400)
pālus -ī m.	wooden stake (6.247, 267)
pānis -is m.	bread (14.128, 181)

panniculus -ī *m.*	scrap of cloth (6.260)
*pār, paris	equal (15.53), the same (14.17)
parātus -a -um	ready (6.16, 245, 273)
parātus -ūs *m.*	service (14.13)
*parcō, parcere, pepercī	spare, go easy on (6.37, 14.215)
parcus -a -um	thrifty, frugal (14.112)
*parens, parentis *m.*	parent (6.13, 14.3, 9, 210)
Paris, Paridis *m.*	Paris (6.87)
pariter *adverb*	together (6.20)
*parō, parāre, parāvī, parātum	prepare (6.26, 251), buy (14.140), construct (14.88), get (14.200)
*pars, partis *f.*	part (14.94, 106, 15.85), serving (14.131), side (15.73)
Parthus -a -um	Parthian (6.407)
particula -ae *f.*	small piece (15.79)
parvulus -a -um	tiny (6.89)
*parvus -a -um	small (6.2, 288, 14.5, 93)
pascō, pascere, pāvī, pastum	feed (14.80)
passer, passeris *m.*	sparrow (6.8)
pateō, patēre, patuī	gape open (6.31)
*pater, patris *m.*	father (6.51, 77, 14.96, 99, 105, 119, 167, 191)
paternus -a -um	fatherly (6.55, 57, 88), ancestral (6.355)
*patior, patī, passus sum	suffer (6.292, 14.161)
*patria -ae *f.*	native land (6.86, 111, 14.166)
patrimōnium -ī *n.*	estate, fortune (14.116, 229)
*paucus -a -um	few (6.50, 15.54), scanty (14.155)
*paulātim *adverb*	gradually (6.19)
*pauper, pauperis	poor (6.72, 14.121)
paupertās -ātis *f.*	poverty (6.295, 358)
pavidus -a -um	fearful, trembling (6.95)
*pax, pācis *f.*	peace (6.292)
pectō, pectere, pexī, pexum	comb (6.27)
pectus, pectoris *n.*	heart (6.93, 96, 251)
*pecūnia -ae *f.*	money (6.298, 14.139)
pecus, pecoris *n.*	flock (6.4)
pēior, pēius	worse (6.270)
pelagus -ī *n.*	sea (6.90)
Pēleus, Pēleī *m.*	Peleus (14.214)

pellis -is *f.*	hide, skin (6.7, 14.187)
penes *prep.+acc.*	under the control of (14.226)
***per** prep.+acc.*	on (6.17), over (6.52), through (6.78, 102, 14.75, 186, 15.56, 92), by means of (14.135, 229), during (14.222), over (15.63)
per sē	on their own (6.244)
percutiō, percutere, percussī, percussum	strike (15.66)
peregrīnus -a -um	foreign (6.298, 14.187)
***pereō, perīre, periī, peritum**	perish (6.295, 362), be done for (6.44)
perferō, perferre, pertulī, perlātum	perform (6.261), endure (6.93)
perfundō, perfundere, perfūdī, perfūsum	mingle (6.303)
pergō, pergere, perrexī, perrectum	move, advance (14.122)
***perīclum -ī** n.*	danger (6.94)
periūrium -ī n.	perjury, false oath (14.218)
perlegō, perlegere, perlēgī, perlectum	study (14.192)
pērō, pērōnis m.	boot (14.186)
persōna -ae f.	mask (6.70)
pertundō, pertundere, pertudī, pertūsum	pierce, lance (6.46)
pervigil, pervigilis	awake all night (15.43)
pervolō, pervolāre, pervolāvī, pervolātum	fly around (6.398)
***pēs, pedis** m.	foot (14.219)
***petō, petere, petīvī, petītum**	source, seek out (14.89)
petulans, petulantis	unruly, insolent (6.297)
Pharos -ī f.	Pharos (6.83)
phrenēsis -is f.	madness (14.136)
piget, pigēre, piguit	it is displeasing (14.199)
pignus, pignoris n.	pledge (6.27)
pilōsus -a -um	hairy (14.194)
pinna -ae f.	wing (14.76)
placeō, placēre (+reflexive pronoun)	be proud of oneself (6.276)
***placeō, placēre, placuī, placitum**	be pleasing (6.33, 38)
plāga -ae f.	blow, stroke (14.19)
planta -ae f.	foot (6.96)
Plēbēia -ōrum n.pl.	Plebeian (games: 6.69)
***plēnus -a -um**	full (6.364, 14.138, 15.58)

plōrō, plōrāre, plōrāvī, plōrātum	weep (6.86, 272, 14.150)
plūma -ae *f.*	feather (6.88)
plūrēs -ēs -a	more in number (14.173)
plūrimus -a -um	very many (14.1, 15.78)
plūs *adverb*	more (6.251, 14.201)
poēta -ae *m.*	poet (14.206)
Polyphēmus -ī *m.*	Polyphemus (14.20)
pōmum -ī *n.*	apple (6.18)
pondus, ponderis *n.*	weight (6.262, 15.66)
*pōnō, pōnere, posuī, positum	serve up (14.83), cast off (6.264, 14.99, 216), set (6.359, 14.203), set up (15.42)
*pons, pontis *m.*	bridge (6.32, 14.134)
Ponticus -a -um	of the Black Sea (14.114)
poples, poplitis *m.*	knee (6.263)
*populus -ī *m.*	people (6.410, 14.115, 160, 15.31, 39)
porrigō, porrigere, porrexī, porrectum	stretch out (6.43)
porrum -ī *n.*	leek (14.133)
*porta -ae *f.*	gate (6.409)
porticus -ūs *f.*	colonnade (6.60)
*poscō, poscere, poposcī	apply for (14.193)
Posīdēs -is *m.*	Posides (14.91)
possideō, possidēre, possēdī, possessum	possess (14.159)
*possum, posse, potuī	be able (6.30, 41, 62, 96, 252, 282, 399, 14.27, 150, 200, 211)
*post *prep.+acc.*	after (14.183, 190)
posthāc	afterwards (14.158)
postis -is *m.*	door-post (6.52, 79)
*postquam *conjunction*	after (15.72)
Postumus -ī *m.*	Postumus (6.21, 28)
*potius	rather (6.398)
pōtō, pōtāre, pōtāvī, pōtātum	drink (6.9)
*praebeō, praebēre, praebuī, praebitum	offer (6.3, 32)
praeceptum -ī *n.*	teaching (14.189)
praecipiō, praecipere, praecēpī, praeceptum	instruct (14.16, 227)
praecipitō, praecipitāre, praecipitāvī, praecipitātum	hurry on, accelerate (15.78)
*praeda -ae *f.*	prey (14.82, 85)

praeferō, praeferre, praetulī, praelātum	prefer (6.111)
praegnās, praegnātis	pregnant (6.405)
Praenestīnus -a -um	of Praeneste (14.88)
praepūtium -ī *n.*	foreskin (14.99)
praesens, praesentis	present (6.400)
praestō, praestāre, praestitī, praestātum	show (6.97, 252), produce (6.287), guarantee (14.212), present (backs in retreat: 15.75)
*praeter *prep.+acc.*	except (14.97)
*praetereā *adverb*	besides (6.107)
praetereō, praeterīre, praeterīvī, praeteritum	surpass (14.214)
prandeō, prandēre, prandī, pransum	eat lunch (6.101)
premō, premere, pressī, pressum	throttle (14.221)
*pretium -ī *n.*	price (14.145)
prīmōrēs -um *m.pl.*	chiefs, leading men (15.40)
prīmum *adverb*	first (14.85)
*prīmus -a -um	first (6.24, 298, 408, 15.51, 90)
principium -ī *n.*	opening speech (6.245)
*prius...quam	before (14.148)
*prō *prep.+abl.*	as reward for (14.163)
prōdigium -ī *n.*	monstrosity (6.84)
prōdigus -a -um	extravagant (6.362)
prōdūcō, prōdūcere, prōduxī, prōductum	rear, bring up (14.228), produce, bring about (15.32)
*proelium -ī *n.*	fight (6.258), battle (14.162)
prōferō, prōferre, prōtulī, prōlātum	extend (14.142), bring about (6.23)
prōgeniēs -ēī *f.*	offspring (14.84)
Promētheus -eos *m.*	Prometheus (15.85)
prōmō, prōmere, prompsī, promptum	bring out (15.73)
prōnus -a -um	lying face down (6.48)
properō, properāre, properāvī, properātum	hurry, hasten (14.78, 178)
propinquus -ī *m.*	relative, relation (14.6)
proprius -a -um	one's own (14.80)
*propter *prep.+acc.*	for the sake of (6.104, 14.22)
prorsus *adverb*	absolutely (6.249)
prospiciō, prospicere, prospexī, prospectum	look ahead (6.360)
prōtinus *adverb*	at once, immediately (14.123)

*proximus -a -um	very close (6.290)
pudet, pudēre, puduit *impersonal vb.*	it is embarrassing (14.185)
Pudīcitia -ae *f.*	Chastity (6.1, 14)
pudīcus -a -um	modest, respectable (6.49)
*pudor -ōris *m.*	decency (6.252, 14.178), shame (6.357)
*puella -ae *f.*	girl (6.258, 14.209), slave-girl (6.354)
*puer, puerī *m.*	son (6.111, 404, 14.3, 11, 192, 228), slave-boy (6.272), boy (14.180, 208)
puerilis -e	boyish (15.59)
*pugna -ae *f.*	fight (15.74)
pugnus -ī *m.*	fist (15.58)
pullulō, pullulāre, pullulāvī, pullulātum	sprout, grow (6.363)
pullus -ī *m.*	chick (14.74)
pulpitum -ī *n.*	wooden platform (6.78)
puls, pultis *f.*	porridge (14.171)
Pūnicus -a -um	Punic, Carthaginian (14.161)
puppis -is *f.*	ship (6.102)
purpura -ae *f.*	purple cloth (14.188)
pusillus -a -um	tiny (14.29, 15.70)
pūsio -ōnis *m.*	boy (6.34–5)
putō, putāre, putāvī, putātum	think (6.34, 41, 14.223, 15.82), believe (14.17, 98, 115, 121)
putris -e	rotting (14.132)
Pyrrha -ae *f.*	Pyrrha (15.30)
Pyrrhus -ī *m.*	Pyrrhus (14.162)
quā	where (14.167)
*quaerō, quaerere, quaesīvī, quaesītum	look for (6.46, 14.76, 104, 181, 15.63), ask (14.207, 15.89)
*quālis -e	what sort of (6.255, 15.65)
quāliscumque, quālecumque	of whatever quality (15.49)
*quam	than (6.398, 14.113, 154, 175)
*quam	how (6.263, 14.150, 152)
*quamquam	although (6.88, 15.30)
quamvīs	although (6.93)
*quandō	when? (6.267)
quantī *genitive of price*	how much (6.365), as much (14.160)
quantulus -a -um	how tiny (6.254)

quantum *adverb*	as much as (6.37, 14.139, 15.45)
*quantus -a -um	how great (6.262)
*quattuor	four (14.168)
*-que	and
quercus -ūs *f.*	oak (i.e. acorns: 14.184)
*queror, querī, questus sum	complain (6.36)
*quī, quae, quod *interrogative adj.*	who, what (6.29, 103, 252, 261, 266, 275, 277, 286, 405–6, 14.152, 177, 221, 15.66–7)
*quī, quae, quod *relative pronoun*	who, which (e.g. 6.12, 35, 44, 62, 73, 76, 100, 104, 112, 242, 248, 253, 259, 282, 301–2, 359, 399)
quīcumque, quaecumque, quodcumque	whoever, whatever (6.355, 412, 14.102, 117, 188, 210, 15.71)
quid quod	what of the fact that (6.45)
*quīdam, quaedam, quiddam	somebody, something (6.55, 409, 14.123, 15.77), some people (6.361, 14.96)
*quidem	admittedly, for sure (15.27)
quīlibet, quaelibet, quodlibet	whatever you please (14.205)
Quintiliānus -ī *m.*	Quintilian (6.75, 280)
quippe	seeing that (6.11, 14.116, 229)
*quis, quid	who, what? (6.41, 58, 104, 247, 300, 359, 402-5, 14.23, 153, 178, 211)
*quisquam, quicquam	anyone (14.6, 15.55)
*quisquis, quidquid	whoever (14.227)
*quō?	what is the point of? (14.135, 15.61)
*quod	that (6.34, 14.114, 15.47), because (15.36, 60, 84)
quondam	at one time (6.288)
*quoque	also (14.79, 127), even (14.108)
*quot	how many? (6.277, 406, 14.151)
*quotiens	whenever (6.67, 14.21)
rādō, rādere, rāsī, rāsum	shave (6.105), peel (14.7)
*rapiō, rapere, rapuī, raptum	sweep along, rush (14.232), seize (15.39, 85)
*ratiō -ōnis *f.*	reason (6.95)
rea -ae *f.*	defendant (6.243)
recēdō, recēdere, recessī, recessum	withdraw, retire (6.19)
*recens, recentis	newly-made (6.11, 408)

recidīvus -a -um	falling back (into the soil: 6.363)
reconditus -a -um	hidden away (6.67)
*rectus -a -um	straight (6.401)
*redeō, redīre, rediī, reditum	come back (14.170)
*referō, referre, rettulī, relātum	report (15.28)
*relinquō, relinquere, relīquī, relictum	leave (14.77), bequeath (14.93), leave behind (6.87, 14.232)
renascor, renascī, renātus sum	grow again (14.11)
reor, rērī, ratus sum	think (15.87)
repetō, repetere, repetīvī, repetītum	return to, recall (15.72)
rēpō, rēpere, rēpsi	crawl (14.208)
reputō, reputāre, reputāvī, reputātum	consider (6.365)
requiēs -ētis f.	retirement (6.106)
requīrō, requīrere, requīsīvī, requīsītum	ask (6.286)
*rēs, reī f.	action (6.97), fortune (14.2), money (6.357), property (6.255, 14.112) wealth (14.92)
respīrō, respīrāre, respīrāvī, respīrātum	draw breath (14.28)
restis -is f.	rope (6.30)
retegō, retegere, retexī, retectum	open up (6.278)
reverentia -ae f.	respect (14.177)
revocō, revocāre, revocāvī, revocātum	call back (14.231)
*rex, rēgis m.	king (6.1, 407)
Rhodos -ī f.	Rhodes (6.296)
rīdeō, rīdēre, rīsī, rīsum	laugh (6.264, 15.71)
rīsus -ūs m.	laughter (6.71)
rixa -ae f.	brawl (15.52)
rixor, rixārī, rixātus sum	fight, scuffle (15.61)
rōbur, rōboris n.	oak-tree (6.12)
*Rōmānus -a -um	Roman (6.295, 14.100, 160)
ruber, rubra, rubrum	red-lettered (14.192)
ructō, ructāre, ructāvī, ructātum	belch (6.10)
rudens, rudentis m.	ship's cable (6.102)
rudis -is f.	wooden sword (6.113, 248)
rūmor, rūmōris m.	gossip, rumour (6.408)
*rumpō, rumpere, rūpī, ruptum	break open (6.12, 14.85, 15.57)

*rūs, rūris *n.*	countryside estate (6.55, 14.141, 155), country district (14.75, 182)
rusticus -a -um	from the countryside, clod-hopping (6.66), naïve (14.25)
Rutilus -ī *m.*	Rutilus (14.18)
sabbata -ōrum *n.pl.*	sabbath (14.96)
sacculus -ī *m.*	purse (14.138)
sacer, sacra, sacrum	sacred (6.22)
sacrum -ī *n.*	religious rite (14.103)
saeculum -ī *n.*	era (6.24, 299)
*saepe *adverb*	often (6.10, 14.174)
saeviō, saevīre, saeviī, saevītum	behave savagely (14.18, 15.54)
*saevus -a -um	ferocious (6.292, 14.148, 175)
sagitta -ae *f.*	arrow (15.74)
saltātus -ūs *m.*	dancing (15.49)
saltō, saltāre, saltāvī, saltātum	dance (6.63)
saltus -ūs *m.*	glade (14.82)
salvus -a -um	safe, available (6.30)
sānābilis -e	able to be cured (15.34)
sānē *adverb*	certainly (15.44, 61)
*sanguis, sanguinis *m.*	blood (14.164, 15.58, 92)
sānus -a -um	sane (6.28)
*satis	enough (14.182)
Saturnus -ī *m.*	Saturn (6.1)
saturō, saturāre, saturāvī, saturātum	feed fully (14.166)
saxum -ī *n.*	rock (15.63)
scaphium -ī *n.*	woman's chamber-pot (6.264)
*scelus, sceleris *n.*	crime (14.173, 188, 224, 15.29–30, 89)
scilicet *adverb*	evidently (14.156)
*scrībō, scrībere, scrīpsī, scriptum	write (14.192)
scrīnium -ī *n.*	book-box (6.278)
scriptum -ī *n.*	writing (6.277)
scrobis -is *m.*	ditch (14.170)
*scūtum -ī *n.*	shield (6.248)
*sē, suī	oneself (6.32, 244, 358, 365, 14.6, 83, 15.59)
secō, secāre, secuī, sectum	cut (6.106, 14.155, 15.78)
sēcrētum -ī *n.*	secret (6.403)

secta -ae *f.*   code of behaviour (14.122)

sectīvus -a -um   chopped (14.133)

sēcūrus -a -um   free of worries (6.62, 14.213)

*sed   but

sedeō, sedēre, sēdī, sessum   rest, be placed (6.263)

sēditiō -ōnis *f.*   civil strife (15.64)

seges, segetis *f.*   crops (14.143)

segmentātus -a -um   decorated with flounces (6.89)

sella -ae *f.*   sedan-chair (6.353)

*semper   always (6.109, 268, 273, 364, 14.14, 118,
                                                  205)

*senātor -ōris *m.*   senator (6.82)

senescō, senescere, senuī   grow feeble with age (6.59)

*senex, senis *m.*   old man (14.4, 181)

*sententia -ae *f.*   thought (14.205)

sentīna -ae *f.*   bilge-water (6.99)

*sentiō, sentīre, sensī, sensum   be aware of (6.362, 15.42), taste (15.90)

September, Septembris *m.*   September (14.130)

*septimus -a -um   seventh (14.10, 105, 15.44)

*sequor, sequī, secūtus sum   follow, accompany (6.100)

Sēres, Sērum *m.pl.*   the Chinese (6.403)

Sergiolus -ī *m.*   Sergiolus ('little Sergius': 6.105)

Sergius -ī *m.*   Sergius (6.112)

sermō, sermōnis *m.*   talking (14.152)

serpens, serpentis *m./f.*   snake (14.74, 114)

*servō, servāre, servāvī, servātum   observe (law: 14.101), protect (14.113),
                                                  save up (14.129)

*servus -ī *m.*   slave (6.279, 14.16, 126)

sevērus -a -um   severe (14.110)

sexagēsimus -a -um   sixtieth (14.197)

sexus -ūs *m.*   sex, gender (6.253)

*sī   if

sī quis, sī quid   someone, something (6.250)

*sīc *adverb*   in this way (14.31, 92, 211)

siccus -a -um   dry (6.401)

*sīcut   as if (6.65)

signō, signāre, signāvī, signātum   lock up (14.132)

silūrus -ī *m.*   catfish (14.132)

silvester, silvestris, silvestre   of the woodland (6.5)

*similis -e	similar (6.7)
simulō, simulāre, simulāvī, simulātum	feign, pretend (6.271)
simultās -ātis f.	feud (15.33)
*sine prep.+abl.	without (15.54)
*sinister, sinistra, sinistrum	on the left side (6.256), harmful (14.1)
*sinō, sinere, sīvī, situm	allow (6.288)
Sīrēn, Sīrēnis f.	Siren (14.19)
sōdēs colloquial	please (6.280)
*sōl, sōlis m.	sun (15.44)
*solitus -a -um	accustomed to, in the habit of (14.100, 129)
*sōlus -a -um	alone, only (6.68, 14.104, 107, 159, 15.37)
*solvō, solvere, soluī, solūtum	undo, open (6.73), loosen (14.199)
*somnus -ī m.	sleep (6.289, 14.222)
sonō, sonāre, sonuī, sonitum	be noisy (6.68, 92, 15.51)
sordēs -is f.	meanness (14.124)
*soror, sorōris f.	sister (6.20, 85, 111)
sortior, sortīrī, sortītus sum	get by chance (14.96)
spadō -ōnis m.	eunuch (14.91)
speciēs -ēī f.	appearance (14.109)
spectāculum -ī n.	show (6.61)
*spectō, spectāre, spectāvī, spectātum	watch (6.352)
spēlunca -ae f.	cave (6.3, 59)
*spērō, spērāre, spērāvī, spērātum	hope for (6.106, 14.6)
sponsālia -ium n.pl.	betrothal ceremony (6.25)
sponte adverb	of their own accord (14.107)
spūmō, spūmāre, spūmāvī, spūmātum	foam (6.303)
statiō -ōnis f.	station (6.274)
sternō, sternere, strāvī, strātum	strew (6.5)
stillō, stillāre, stillāvī, stillātum	drip (6.109)
stimulō, stimulāre, stimulāvī, stimulātum	goad, drive on (14.84)
*stō, stāre, stetī, statum	stand (6.291, 15.91)
stomachus -ī m.	stomach (6.100)
strepitus -ūs m.	noise (14.19)
strīdor -ōris m.	clanking sound (14.23)
*stultus -a -um	stupid (6.43)
stupeō, stupēre, stupuī	be astounded (6.87)
suādeō, suādēre, suāsī, suāsum (+dative)	urge (14.23, 225)
*sub prep.+abl.	under the rule of (6.15, 14.160)

subeō, subīre, subiī, subitum	come upon (14.33, 202), walk under (14.221)
*subitō	suddenly (6.65)
subligar -āris *n.*	actor's loincloth (6.70)
subsidium -ī *n.*	reinforcements (15.73)
subsīdō, subsīdere, subsēdī	collapse (6.411)
subsistō, subsistere, substitī	halt (14.231)
sudō, sudāre, sudāvī, sudātum	sweat (6.259)
sufficiō, sufficere, suffēcī, suffectum	be enough (6.53, 14.141, 172, 15.80)
suillus -a -um	pork (14.98)
sulcus -ī *m.*	furrow (6.107, 14.170)
*sum, esse, fuī	be
summa -ae *f.*	sum of money (14.218)
summoveō, summovēre, summōvī, summōtum	deflect (14.186)
*summus -a -um	topmost, highest (6.99, 14.87, 15.85), greatest (15.35)
*sūmō, sūmere, sūmpsī, sūmptum	pick up (6.264, 266), put on (14.76), derive, draw (6.285)
super *prep.+acc.*	beyond (15.28)
superī -ōrum *m.pl.*	gods above (6.19)
*supersum, superesse, superfuī	be left (6.355)
supīnus -a -um	lying on one's back (14.190)
sustineō, sustinēre, sustinuī	endure (6.105, 14.127, 15.88)
*suus -a -um	one's own (6.274, 14.112)
Sybaris -is *f.*	Sybaris (6.296)
syrma -atis *n.*	actor's robe (15.30)
tabella -ae *f.*	writing-tablet (6.277)
*tālis -e	of such a kind (14.150, 166, 210, 225)
*tam	so (14.27)
*tamen	but, however (6.25, 55, 58, 103, 253, 286, 355, 359, 14.93, 107, 226, 15.59)
tamquam	as though (14.111–2)
*tandem	finally, at last (6.361, 14.163)
*tangō, tangere, tetigī, tactum	touch (14.219)
*tantus -a -um	so much (14.27, 159), so great (15.89)
tardus -a -um	slow (15.82)
Tarentum -ī *n.*	Tarentum (6.297)
Tarpēius -a -um	Tarpeian (6.47)

Tatius -ī *m.*	Tatius (14.160)
*tectum -ī *n.*	dwelling (6.289), ceiling (6.304)
*tēcum	with you (6.34)
tegimen, tegiminis *n.*	covering (6.257)
*tegō, tegere, texī, tectum	protect (14.186), conceal (6.44)
Telamōn -ōnis *m.*	Telamon (14.214)
*tēlum -ī *n.*	weapon (15.53, 65)
*tempestās -ātis *f.*	time, era (6.26)
*templum -ī *n.*	temple (15.42)
*tempus, temporis *n.*	time (14.130, 157, 15.38, 68)
tendō, tendere, tetendī, tentum	stretch out (6.52)
*teneō, tenēre, tenuī, tentum	hold (6.70), grip (6.410)
tener, tenera, tenerum	young, tender (14.215)
Tentyra -ōrum *n.pl.*	Tentyra (15.35, 76)
tenuis -e	thin (6.259)
ter	three times (14.28)
*tergum -ī *n.*	back (15.75)
*terra -ae *f.*	earth (6.2, 14.7, 15.70, 86, 92), land (6.411, 14.222)
testis -is *m.*	witness (14.218)
testūdineus -a -um	overlaid with tortoise-shell (6.80)
theātrum -ī *n.*	theatre (6.68)
Thrax, Thrācis *m.*	Thracian (6.403)
Thymelē -ēs *f.*	Thymele (6.66)
thyrsus -ī *m.*	ritual staff, thyrsus (6.70)
Tiberis -is *m.*	Tiber (14.202)
tībīcen, tībīcinis *m.*	pipe-player (15.49)
Tibur, Tiburis *n.*	Tibur (14.87)
tigris -idis *f.*	female tiger (6.270)
*timeō, timēre, timuī	fear (6.17), be nervous of (6.51), be afraid (6.95)
Tīsiphonē -ēs *f.*	Tisiphone (6.29)
titubō, titubāre, titubāvī, titubātum	totter (15.48)
*tollō, tollere, sustulī, sublātum	bring up (6.38), take (6.364)
tonsor -ōris *m.*	barber (6.26)
tormentum -ī *n.*	torment, torture (14.135)
torqueō, torquēre, torsī, tortum	hurl, throw (15.64)
tortor, tortōris *m.*	torturer (14.21)
torus -ī *m.*	bed (6.5, 15.43)

*tot	so many (6.30, 15.61)
totidem	as many again (14.13)
totiens *adverb*	so often (6.44, 94)
*tōtus -a -um	entire (6.61, 14.148, 15.80, 91), the whole of, all (6.398, 402, 14.94, 154, 230, 15.55)
tractō, tractāre, tractāvī, tractātum	handle (6.102)
*trādō, trādere, trādidī, trāditum	hand down (14.3, 102)
tragicus -ī *m.*	tragedian (15.31)
tragoedus -ī *m.*	tragic actor (6.74)
transeō, transīre, transiī, transitum	pass by (14.11)
tremulus -a -um	trembling (6.96)
trepidus -a -um	terrified (14.20, 199)
*trēs, tria	three (14.169)
*tristis -e	unhappy (6.69), gloomy (14.110)
trivium -ī *n.*	crossroads (6.412)
*tū, tuī *pronoun*	you (*singular*) (e.g. 6.7, 32, 49, 60, 258, 275–6, 282)
tuba -ae *f.*	trumpet (6.250, 15.52)
tūber terrae, tūberis terrae *n.*	truffle (14.7)
Tuccia -ae *f.*	Tuccia (6.64)
*tum	then (6.270)
tunc	at that time (6. 11), then (6.66, 270), in that case (6.99, 276, 14.21)
tunica -ae *f.*	pod (of a lupin: 14.153)
*turba -ae *f.*	crowd (14.167), mob (15.46, 61, 81)
turbō, turbāre, turbāvī, turbātum	upset (6.8), fritter away (14.94)
turgeō, turgēre, tursī	swell (14.138)
Turnus -ī *m.*	Turnus (15.65)
turpis -e	disgraceful (6.299)
turpiter *adverb*	disgracefully (6.97)
turris -is *f.*	tower (6.291)
turtur, turturis *m.*	turtle-dove (6.39)
Tuscus -a -um	Etruscan (6.289)
tūtēla -ae *f.*	guardian, protector (14.112)
*tuus -a -um	your (6.61, 14.205)
Tȳdīdēs -ae *m.*	son of Tydeus (Diomedes: 15.66)
Tyrius -a -um	Tyrian (6.246)
Tyrrhēnus -a -um	Etruscan (6.92)

ūber, ūberis *n.*	breast (6.9)
ūber, ūberis	overflowing (6.273)
ulciscor, ulciscī, ultus sum	wreak revenge on (6.293)
*ullus -a -um	any (6.30, 41, 14.106, 145, 174, 202)
*ultimus -a -um	last (15.90)
ultrā *prep.+acc.*	beyond (14.202)
umbra -ae *f.*	gloom (6.4), semblance (14.109)
umbrōsus -a -um	shady (15.76)
*umquam	ever (6.266, 365, 14.127, 165, 178, 15.88)
*unde	from where? (6.286, 14.207)
unguentum -ī *n.*	perfume, scent (6.303, 14.204, 15.50)
*ūnus -a -um	one (6.53–4, 14.141, 168, 15.79)
Urbicus -ī *m.*	Urbicus (6.71)
*urbs, urbis *f.*	city (6.84, 290, 398, 411)
ūrō, ūrere, ussī, ustum	burn (6.260), brand (14.22)
Ursidius -ī *m.*	Ursidius (6.38, 42)
ūrūca -ae *f.*	worm (6.276)
usque adeō	to such an extent (15.82)
*ut *(+subjunctive)*	that (6.54, 75, 14.25, 121), so that (6.87, 14.16, 149, 15.79)
*ut *(+indicative)*	as (6.56, 14.213–14)
*uterque, utraque, utrumque	both, each of two (15.37)
ūtilis -e	useful (6.359)
utrimque	on both sides (15.35)
*uxor, uxōris *f.*	wife (6.5, 28, 45, 76, 267, 14.168)
vacuus -a -um	empty (6.68)
*valeō, valēre, valuī, valītum	be strong (6.100), be strong enough to (15.67)
vānus -a -um	foolish, silly (14.211)
vāsum -ī *n.*	vase (6.356)
Vēiiento -ōnis *m.*	Veiiento (6.113)
*vel	or (6.247, 257, 286, 14.132, 162, 170, 15.66)
vellus, velleris *n.*	fleece (6.289)
vēlox, vēlōcis	swift (14.31)
*velut	as though (6.363)
vēna -ae *f.*	vein (6.46)

vēnālis -e	for sale (14.151)
vendō, vendere, vendidī, venditum	sell (6.258, 14.200, 218)
venēnum -ī *n.*	poison (14.173)
vēnor, vēnārī, vēnātus sum	hunt (14.82)
venter, ventris *m.*	stomach (14.126), belly (14.149), bowels (14.199)
venus, veneris *f.*	sexual desire (6.300)
*verbum -ī *n.*	word (6.406)
vernula -ae *m.*	home-born slave (14.169)
verpus -a -um	circumcised (14.104)
versō, versāre, versāvī, versātum	turn over, dwell on (14.206)
vertīgō, vertīginis *f.*	dizzying motion (6.304)
*vertō, vertere, vertī, versum	spin (6.99)
veru -ūs *n.*	roasting-spit (15.82)
*vērus -a -um	real (6.251)
vēsīca -ae *f.*	bladder, vagina (6.64)
*vester, vestra, vestrum	your (14.220)
vestigium -ī *n.*	trace (6.14)
Vestīnus -a -um	of the Vestini tribe (14.181)
*vestis -is *f.*	clothing (6.352, 14.110)
*vetō, vetāre, vetuī, vetitum	prevent (6.74), forbid (14.185)
vetulus -a -um	elderly (14.208)
*vetus, veteris	ancient (6.14, 21), old (14.184, 189), long-standing (15.33)
vexātus -a -um	chafed (6.290)
*via -ae *f.*	way (14.103), route (14.122, 223)
vice (+*genitive*)	in place of (15.53)
vīcīnia -ae *f.*	neighbourhood (14. 154)
vīcīnus -a -um	neighbouring (6.32, 14.143, 15.76)
vīcīnus -ī *m./f.*	a neighbour (6.6, 15.36)
*victōria -ae *f.*	victory (15.47)
victrix, victricis *f.*	victorious (15.81)
vīcus -ī *m.*	street (6.78)
*videō, vidēre, vīdī, vīsum	see (6.2, 24, 104, 247, 408)
*videor, vidērī, vīsus sum	look like (6.113), seem (14.142, 165, 15.40)
vidua -ae *f.*	widow (6.405)
vigilō, vigilāre, vigilāvī, vigilātum	stay awake (14. 192)
*villa -ae	villa (14.89, 95, 141)

*vincō, vincere, vīcī, victum	defeat (6.293), surpass (14.90–1, 213–14), win over (14.145)
violō, violāre, violāvī, violātum	pollute (15.84)
*vir, virī *m.*	man (6.53, 254, 360, 399, 15.48), husband (6.112, 270)
vīrēs, vīrium *f.pl.*	strength (6.253)
virgō, virginis *f.*	unmarried girl (14.29)
viridis -e	lush, green (14.147)
*virtūs, virtūtis *f.*	virtue (14.109)
*vīta -ae *f.*	life (14.106, 157)
vītis -is *f.*	vine-staff (14.193)
vitium -ī *n.*	immoral behaviour (6.288, 14.32), vice (14.109, 123, 175)
vitta -ae *f.*	chaplet, woollen band (6.50)
*vīvō, vīvere, vīxī, vīctum	live (6.12, 18, 56–7, 14.137, 179, 15.62)
*vīvus -a -um	alive, living (15.69)
*vix	scarcely (14.150, 163, 15.55)
*vocō, vocāre, vocāvī, vocātum	summon (14.21)
*volō, velle, voluī	wish, want (6.282, 14.176–7, 185)
volūmen, volūminis *n.*	scroll, book (14.102)
voluptās -ātis *f.*	pleasure (6.254, 15.90)
volvō, volvere, voluī, volūtum	read, unwind (15.30)
*vōs, vestrī *pronoun*	you (*plural*: 6.265)
vōtum -ī *n.*	heart's desire (6.60, 14.125)
vulgus -ī *n.*	mob, crowd (15.29, 36)
*vulnus, vulneris *n.*	injury (6.247, 14.164, 15.34, 54)
vultur, vulturis *m.*	vulture (14.77, 79)
*vultus -ūs *m.*	face (14.110, 15.56)
zēlotypus -a -um	jealous (6.278)